The Couple's Guide to Thriving with ADHD

MELISSA ORLOV

Author of *The ADHD Effect on Marriage*

NANCIE KOHLENBERGER, LMFT

Specialty Press, Inc.

300 N.W. 70th Ave., Suite 102

Plantation, Florida 33317

Book Design and Layout: Babs Kall, Kall Graphics

Melissa Orlov's photo by Steve Robb
Nancie Kohlenberger's photo by Pamela Novillo

Specialty Press, Inc.
300 Northwest 70th Avenue, Suite 102
Plantation, Florida 33317
(954) 792-8100 • (800) 233-9273

Printed in the United States of America

Library of Congress Cataloging-in-Publication Data

Orlov, Melissa.
The couple's guide to thriving with ADHD / Melissa Orlov, Nancie Kohlenberger, LMFT.
pages cm
Summary: "More and more often, adults are realizing that the reason they are struggling so much in their relationship is that they are impacted by previously undiagnosed adult ADHD. The Couple's Guide to Thriving with ADHD gives concrete answers and strategies to those suffering from adult ADHD that couples can immediately use to improve their relationships. This book addresses questions from both ADHD and non-ADHD partners and provides straightforward advice arranged in a way that makes it easy to find the specific answers couples seek. It covers topics that include diagnosing adult ADHD, how to begin bringing about changes, communication techniques, dealing with anger and frustration, and rebuilding intimacy in a relationship. Part reference manual and part cheerleader, this is the go-to book for couples struggling with ADHD who want to actively work to improve their relationships"-- Provided by publisher.

ISBN 978-1-937761-10-3 (paperback)

1. Attention-deficit disorder in adults. 2. Couples--Psychology. I. Kohlenberger, Nancie, 1953- II. Title.

RC394.A85O76 2014

616.85'89--dc23

2014004079

Praise for *The Couple's Guide to Thriving with ADHD*

"A book destined to save marriages in trouble and awaken those in repose. Orlov has 'been there and done that,' which, along with her naturalist's eye and ear for the telling detail, makes this manual a rich and friendly foray into the wilds of ADHD. No need any longer for white knuckles; Orlov and Kohlenberger show you how to create a smooth ride in turbulent air."

Edward Hallowell, M.D., of The Hallowell Centers in Sudbury, MA, New York and San Francisco

"Hands down the best book for couples dealing with ADHD. No other book comes even close to providing a balance of the positives, negatives and all that is between: "Thrive" provides both inspiration and concrete strategies for couples learning to find joy again after years of struggling with ADHD. I love this book!"

Bryan Hutchinson, Author of *7 Crucial Tips for Parents and Teachers of Children with ADHD*

"As in Ms. Orlov's ground-breaking first book, *The ADHD Effect on Marriage,* Orlov and Nancie Kohlenberger here provide extremely helpful insights, practical advice, and sage wisdom for couples in which one or both partners have ADHD. This new book, *The Couple's Guide to Thriving with ADHD,* focuses on the "hot spots" which typically engender distress, such as those related to communication, dealing with anger, and navigating chores and tasks at home. Written in a compassionate, understanding tone, as though they were speaking directly to the couple, the aim of this book is not to help couples merely cope with ADHD but to thrive, re-igniting the spark of love and romance that brought them together in the first place."

Mary Solanto, Ph.D., Associate Professor, Director, ADHD Center, Icahn School of Medicine at Mount Sinai. Author of *Cognitive-Behavioral Therapy for Adult ADHD: Targeting Executive Dysfunction*

"This book is a must-read for couples who want a healthy, loving relationship. Written for both the reader with ADD/ADHD and without, *The Couple's Guide to Thriving with ADHD* does an excellent job of explaining the intricate ways ADHD can affect couples.

Easy to read, the authors offer an insightful look at the most common 'hot-spots' (both obvious and subtle) that couples need to recognize and work through, in order to maintain and strengthen their relationship.

The book does more than provide a better understanding of ADHD and its effect on couples. It digs deeper, to offer invaluable, practical tips and techniques for dealing with those issues. This is a guidebook to a happier, healthier relationship. It will help reduce stress and bring back the affection and romance that often gets lost in the struggles of ADHD."

Harold Meyer, Coach & Executive Director,
The A.D.D. Resource Center
Chair, CHADD of New York City

"A wonderful guide to the unique ways that ADHD can impact relationships. Partners will learn that they are not alone in their struggles, and what it takes to adapt and enjoy life with each other to the fullest. The authors have created a frank, practical and bravely personal guide that will help many."

Craig Surman M.D., Scientific Coordinator,
Adult ADHD Research Program, Massachusetts
General Hospital; Assistant Professor of
Psychiatry, Harvard Medical School; Co-author of
FAST MINDS: How to Thrive if You Have ADHD

"As a late-diagnosed woman with ADHD, I can attest to the hopelessness engendered by a lifetime of inexplicable failure and heartbreak. *The Couple's Guide to Thriving with ADHD* offers hope when all seems lost. It achieves what Hollywood-inspired visions of romance cannot: a practical roadmap to relationship recovery that is truly sustainable and offers a real-life happy ending.

Authors Orlov and Kohlenberger, armed with their collective professional and personal experience with ADHD in marriage, are not offering a fairytale in The Couple's Guide to Thriving with ADHD. Without shying away from the negative impact of ADHD symptoms, they offer something much more valuable: a script away from blame and back to a partnership with the chance of a real-life happily-ever-after."

Zoë Kessler, B.A., B.Ed., Author of *ADHD According to Zoë – The Real Deal on Relationships, Finding Your Focus & Finding Your Keys*

Practical, accessible, compassionate, and a pleasure to read … a must-have book for any couple living with the challenges and rewards of ADHD. It offers strategies to regain a positive and long-lasting loving relationship. The perfect life companion for couples and coaches who deal with ADHD on a daily basis.

Nancy Ratey, ED.M., MCC, BCC Author, *The Disorganized Mind*

"Compassionate, concise, and insightful, *The Couple's Guide to Thriving with ADHD* is filled with 'a-ha' moments, and is a must-read for consumers and mental health professionals alike. Melissa Orlov continues to impress me as an authoritative voice on ADHD in couples."

Noah Rubinstein, LMFT,
Founder of GoodTherapy.org

"*In The Couple's Guide to Thriving with ADHD*, Orlov and Kohlenberger not only tackle the obvious challenges that ADHD-impacted couples face, like communication and control issues, but they also delve into difficulties that are just as common but often unaddressed, such as the chronic anger that either partner may feel, as well as the parent/child dynamic that many couples find themselves trapped in. Through personal experience, expert knowledge, and kind-hearted compassion, Melissa and Nancie provide ADHD-impacted couples with a thorough understanding of why they are experiencing certain challenges in their relationship, and what they can do to overcome these challenges. Their methods are multi-layered and offer help for all couples—from those who are just beginning their work to those who just need to make a few improvements, and even to those whose partners are not yet ready to make changes.

Melissa Orlov is a popular speaker at the Virtual AD/HD Conference®, and a shining star in the ADHD universe. I highly recommend *The Couple's Guide to Thriving with ADHD*!"

Jennifer Koretsky, SCAC, author of
Odd One Out: The Maverick's Guide to Adult ADD
and Director of the Annual Virtual
AD/HD Conference

This one is in honor of my father, from whom
I've learned so much about how to love generously
and give of myself to others.

—Melissa

I dedicate this in honor of my mom,
who embraced everyone she met with compassion
and kindness and who, through those qualities,
continues to inspire me every day.

— Nancie

Contents

Foreword

I sometimes say that when one person in a couple has ADHD, then both partners kind of "have" it too because it affects both of them. Everything about one person affects the other person in intimate romantic relationships—hopefully mostly in good ways, but also in some negative ways. ADHD doesn't just affect the practical matters of life, such as loading the dishwasher and remembering to call the bank. It also affects the emotional aspects, such as trust, closeness, connection, and empathy. In other words, all the same challenges that every relationship needs to deal with. ADHD affected couples haven't invented new relationship struggles that other couples don't also have to work through—relationships are relationships, no matter who is in them. What the ADHD does is increase the frequency or intensity of the same practical and emotional struggles that the neighbors are also wrestling with—fairness in the division of labor and feeling like the relationship brings out the best in each of the partners.

Creating a happy and enduring relationship is no easy task, but it can feel almost impossible when the couple doesn't know about ADHD—and when I say that they don't know about it, what I mean is that they don't have ADHD as the explanation for it. They will both know very, very well all the ways that ADHD is affecting their lives. But before the word ADHD comes up on their radar screens, they will use other explanations which may begin as neutral or vaguely positive, such as, "he's just a free spirit," but will rather quickly degenerate into decidedly more negative interpretations, such as, "he's only interested in his things." A friend of mine, Stephanie Sarkis, says that ADHD is the worst kept secret. Once you are living with someone and your lives are intimately tied together, it's impossible to hide ADHD. So that's the bad news.

The good news is that once ADHD is diagnosed, a whole new world opens up—not just for the person with ADHD, but for the romantic partner as well. The diagnosis completely changes how they both view these previously unexplainable behaviors. More importantly, it gives them specific action steps they can take to make their lives better—strategies that are far better than all those well-intentioned but short-lived plans that didn't take the ADHD into account and therefore fell short of expectations. The diagnosis of ADHD can also have a tremendous emotional impact for both partners, by changing the perception of the problematic ADHD behaviors as being less a matter of choice (and therefore a reflection of character) and more as a reflection of certain abilities. So with some better strategies, the person with ADHD can more effectively, reliably, and consistently use the rest of their abilities.

But that's not where the story ends. I sometimes say that the neurological drives the psychological—ADHD neurology influences the experiences that someone encounters over the course of their lives which influences their psychology. It impacts how they handle challenges, how they see themselves, and how they relate to other people. But that's not even where the story ends—ADHD also affects how the other person behaves in the relationship. Just as having ADHD leads to some common behaviors and psychological outcomes in the individual with ADHD, it also tends to drive certain common behaviors and psychological outcomes in their romantic partners, as Melissa Orlov has so clearly discussed in *The ADHD Effect on Marriage*.

So this is where it all gets *really* interesting—if both partners can understand how undiagnosed and untreated ADHD has affected both of them, they are in a much stronger position to address it. This goes way beyond the basics like getting the dishwasher loaded more frequently (which is nice but ultimately doesn't make or break relationships). Really understanding how ADHD has affected both partners in the relationship can strengthen the very foundation of that relationship. It changes how both people see themselves and how they see each other. It all makes much more sense now—which makes it much easier to forgive your partner and even yourself. You may still not be happy about how ADHD affected your relationship, and we can't change the past, but we can certainly use this understanding to create a better future. The neurology may remain (although it does respond well to treatment) but the psychology can be completely different.

A good relationship is one that pushes you to become a better person. As much as undiagnosed and untreated ADHD can easily bring out the worst in both partners, understanding the effect that ADHD is having on each of you will enable you both to bring your best. In this much-needed book, Melissa Orlov and Nancie Kohlenberger walk you through the hot spots that are so common in ADHD affected relationships and how to overcome them. You and your partner owe it to the relationship to take this information seriously. You can't choose whether or not you have ADHD, but you do get to choose what to do about it. With the right information, like that found in this important and insightful book, you will be able to create that rewarding relationship that you both deserve and have worked so hard for.

Ari Tuckman, PsyD, MBA

Acknowledgments

I would like to recognize all of the adults who visit my website and share their stories. Whether you are struggling terribly, have successfully turned your relationship around, or are somewhere in between, your willingness to write your questions fires my continued devotion to exploring the issues that face ADHD-impacted couples. Thank you for sharing your lives with so many.

My husband, George, also deserves a big shout out. He often jokes that I "couldn't have done it without him" and it is certainly true that his ADHD has changed my life. But all joking aside, he is an extraordinary man who has made a great deal of effort, particularly in the last 10 years, to help us stay together as friends and lovers. He continues to teach me about appreciating our unique differences and laughing about our foibles. Neither of us does it just right all the time, but his recent comment that "it's all about being able to talk about anything with each other" is spot on. He has grown to be fearless in his willingness to listen and consider my opinions, and I try to do the same for him. Relationships are a journey, and I'm glad I'm on this one with him. Happy 25th anniversary!

Finally, my thanks to the team that helped bring this book to fruition—my publisher, Harvey Parker, who has dedicated a great deal of time and energy to serving the ADHD community, Babs Kall who continues to do wonderful work in graphics, and Kerri Hartman, who edited the book. My continuing and deep appreciation to Dr. Ned Hallowell and Dr. John Ratey, both of whom generously reviewed our chapter on treatment; and last, but certainly not least, my sincere thanks to my terrific co-author, Nancie Kohlenberger. She has been an excellent sounding board for ideas, and a joy to work with.

—Melissa Orlov

I would like to recognize all of the clients who have shared their experiences and challenges with me, and most particularly those whose lives have been touched in one way or another with ADHD. I appreciate the courage, the perseverance, the determination and the inner strength it takes to put one foot in front of the other every day, in order to handle what life puts in front of us, when our brains don't always function exactly as we would like them to. So, to those of you who have shared your stories with me, and gone through trials in your desire to live more successful and fulfilling lives, I say thank you. It continues to be a privilege to work with you.

And, of course, this is also in recognition of my husband Steve, who has supported all my efforts, both large and small. We continue to grow and learn from each other every day. I too, *could not have done this without you!* You are my best teacher on this road called "Life." And every day brings us new adventures. I am so very grateful that we keep moving forward in love.

And, to Tonka and Tobey, my sweet Cavalier King Charles Spaniels, who sit beside me, as I pound away on my laptop, keeping me company with their warming love throughout the process.

And, finally, thanks to all those dedicated to help making this book a reality. Thanks to Harvey and Babs, and of course, Melissa, for choosing me to participate in this amazing journey. Through you, I have learned so much, and I appreciate, beyond words, this incredible opportunity to co-author what I hope will be a wonderful addition to the field of knowledge about ADHD. It has been an honor and a pleasure to work with you. Thanks so very much!

— Nancie Kohlenberger

1

Couples, Emotions, and ADHD

"Do not try to change yourself — you are unlikely to succeed. Work to improve the way you perform."

—Peter Drucker

This book is about emotions—yours...and your partner's. It's about taking a relationship that is more challenging than you'd like it to be, and making it a lot better. It's about shaping your relationship—intentionally—back into one you can enjoy and feel really good about. And it's about learning scientifically-researched techniques that can help you replace emotions such as ambivalence, frustration, and anger with feelings of love, compassion and joy.

We're excited to share this information with you. Positive emotions are what great relationships are all about—and we want to enable you to find what you most treasure about each other and feel those feelings again, putting ADHD to the sidelines where it belongs.

We've seen couple after couple triumph over ADHD-related issues and re-find the love they thought they had lost. We want you to be part of that group.

The Inherent Tension

No discussion of emotions in ADHD-impacted relationships would be complete without pointing out that there are inherent tensions between the very qualities that define one as having ADHD and the qualities that comprise strong relationships. Take a look at the chart below. On the left side are a few common symptoms and behaviors associated with ADHD. On the right are characteristics of healthy relationships.

ADHD Characteristic	Adult Relationship Characteristic
Distracted – variable attention, "immediate" more engaging than "important"	**Attentive, connected, romantic** – the ability to attend to each other or focus on each other at appropriate times; the ability to consistently demonstrate love
Poor organizational or planning skills –difficulty initiating or completing tasks	**Equality, partnership & reliability** – the ability to share responsibility in the relationship, be counted on, manage one's daily functioning
Time management issues – often late; difficulty anticipating duration of projects; gets lost in projects	**Reliability** – is there when expected, completes tasks when expected
Poor memory – forgets conversations, tasks, partner's priorities	**Reliability, caring** – ability to remember issues that are important to your partner, demonstrate that you care, complete tasks as promised
Impulsive – Can act without thinking ahead or considering consequences	**Trust, partnership, reliability** – ability to make considered decisions for the betterment of the couple or family

We are not suggesting that ADHD-impacted relationships can't be strong because this tension exists. We *know* that they can be very strong! We merely want to point out that couples do significantly better when they are aware of this tension and use specific techniques to overcome or moderate it. We call these techniques "treatment" in the broadest possible sense of that word. Treatment is simply what each of you *does* to make yourselves better partners. This whole book is about "treatment" when you look at it that way, and Chapter 2 gives you a specific treatment framework couples have found very useful as they think about how to thrive together.

The Pervasiveness of ADHD

ADHD doesn't go away. Medications and treatments don't cure it; they simply help the ADHD partner manage the symptoms. But most adults can manage the symptoms quite well with work, willpower and time.You will likely need to remain vigilant, but the future can be significantly smoother as you determine the best ways to adapt to the presence of ADHD.

It's important to reiterate that the problems created in your *relationship* by the presence of ADHD are the result of the symptoms and how the two of you together handle those symptoms. We described the symptom/response/response pattern in *The ADHD Effect on Marriage* and want to remind you that properly interpreting ADHD symptoms is an important factor in your success as a couple. For example, knowing that your partner's lack of attention to you is a symptom (distractibility) rather than a signal that he no longer cares, is critical to making the right choice about how to respond (you might schedule time together instead of getting angry or hurt).

But making these choices can be hard to do. First you must learn about the patterns ADHD encourages. Then you must learn how to change them. The transition from being a couple that did not know about ADHD to being one that handles

ADHD so well that it no longer plays much of a role, takes time and effort. During that transition, there are a lot of confusing emotions and questions with which to deal.

Some of these emotional struggles have to do with how long it takes to get ADHD symptomatic behaviors under control. It's hard for non-ADHD partners to understand this process because the experience of having ADHD is so foreign. Like those with ADHD, non-ADHD partners are sometimes distracted, inconsistent, late, forgetful, poor planners and more. However, their view of what it's like to have these characteristics is skewed by the temporary nature of the issues for them. Being chronically distracted and inconsistent, as are those who have ADHD, is an entirely different experience.

Ninety-eight percent of adults with ADHD report they *often* have time management problems, 94% report they often have inhibition problems, 89% report they often have issues with poor mental organization, and the list goes on (Barkley & Benton, 2010, p. 55). These are *chronic* issues, impacting every facet of the ADHD partner's life. But don't stop there...imagine having these issues without knowing about the ADHD! This is the experience most adults with ADHD have had. It is, at a minimum, confusing. Typically, it leads to poor self-esteem, counter-productive coping strategies, a fear of failure, and more. All of these impact the speed with which couples, and ADHD partners in particular, move forward.

Though it can be wonderful to live with someone who has his or her ADHD under control, it can be difficult for ADHD partners to realize how hard it is to live with, and be a partner to, someone with *undiagnosed or untreated* ADHD. Lives that non-ADHD partners and other-ADHD partners previously had fairly well under control are impacted greatly by the unpredictability inherent in ADHD symptomatic behaviors. Non-ADHD partners end up feeling they need to be constantly on alert so their lives don't spiral out of control. ADHD partners, who have learned to live with the impact of ADHD symptoms, are often oblivious to the very real emotional problems and stress their symptoms encourage in their partners.

We suggest you read *The ADHD Effect on Marriage* for much more in-depth information on the patterns ADHD encourages in relationships and the steps couples can take to respond. It will get you started on the road to change. (We're not trying to sell you another book. It's just that *The ADHD Effect* has a lot of valuable information we cannot repeat here. If you like, pick it up at your public library.)

The Couple's Guide to Thriving with ADHD plays a different role than the first book. While the first book identified the impact of adult ADHD on relationships and provided a strategy of attack, this book helps you recognize and navigate the emotional speed bumps you will inevitably encounter on your journey to relationship repair. We've identified 21 of these issues as *Hot Spots*. We then provide ideas about what may be going on and suggest strategies for getting out of these hot spots to calmer, "cooler" ground. We encourage you to approach the task quite deliberately. In fact, we encourage couples to create what we call an *intentional relationship* as they reshape who they are together and integrate ADHD-friendly tactics and responses into their lives.

The Intentional Relationship

In an intentional relationship, both partners think very carefully about their choices and responses. They focus on today and building a tomorrow rather than rehashing past difficulties. They learn all they can about ADHD, its treatment, and how to respond to it. They experiment singly and together. When things don't work as planned, they consider it a *learning experience* rather than a failure, and experiment again—this time honing their efforts a bit.

Each couple progresses at a different rate, and some never make it. But in general, if all goes well, the arc of your relationship recovery will have three stages:

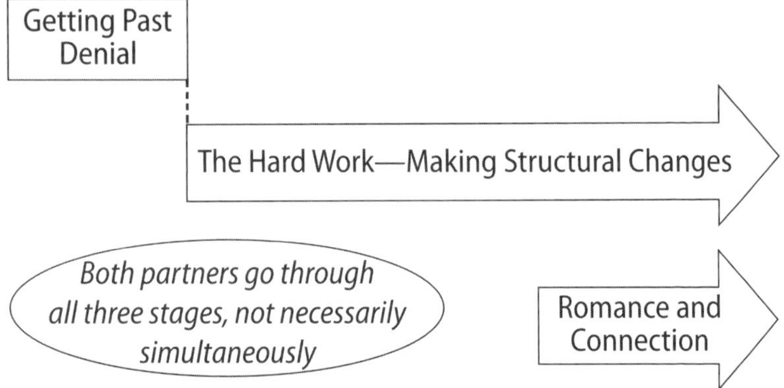

STAGE 1: Overcoming denial and resistance in both partners. In this stage, one or both partners resist the idea that ADHD, or responses to ADHD, might be creating problems in their relationship. There is quite a bit of blaming of the other person, and the *ADHD Effect* patterns are prevalent. This stage ends as both partners become more informed about the impact of ADHD and genuinely agree to start to apply specific tactics to address their own personal issues to better manage ADHD in their lives.

STAGE 2: The hard work—changing your individual and partnership behaviors. In this stage, partners learn to incorporate the three legs of treatment described in Chapter 2 to tame ADHD in their relationship. This stage includes lots of experiments to figure out what treatments and tactics work best for each of you.

STAGE 3: Return of affection and romance. How and when partners start to feel more romantically about each other again varies greatly by couple. Typically, romance returns after both partners have made some visible, sustainable improvements in behavior. Sustained change allows each partner to be seen as more reliable, and therefore *trustworthy*. This increases the likelihood that emotional risks can be taken again, providing an opportunity for affection and romance to bloom.

That's a very dry way of looking at how things might progress in your relationship. Here's the less clinical version: over time, and with great intentionality, the two of you can craft a relationship that is all the richer because you have overcome a significant struggle. You have each learned how to love your partner as the person he or she really is, and can express that love in a way that your partner can hear. You have given the gift of forgiveness to yourself and your partner and created ways to work through even the most difficult subjects. Unlike many other couples, you understand the value of nurturing your relationship over the long haul and keep an eye on whether or not the two of you attend to each other well enough. You have developed a way of talking about problems as they come up.

Most importantly, you have each given great thought to what you love about your partner and made a conscious choice to focus on the positive aspects of who you are and what you each contribute to your relationship. Your choice to stay together is just that—a choice—and you know why you made it.

A relationship impacted by ADHD is not always easy, even after you've revived it…but then again, no relationship *is always easy*. The two of you have learned how to thrive together and understand the tools that you used to build what you have. There is a strength in the relationship that comes from the personal nature of your journey. And that strength, to us, is something to cherish.

So join us on this journey! We welcome feedback, comments, questions and ideas at the www.adhdmarriage.com website, and invite you to check there regularly for information that may help you and your partner find inspiration on your way.

ADHD/ADHD Partnerships

Couples in which both partners have ADHD often find that one partner is more organized than the other and therefore takes on many of the roles described in this book as non-ADHD. So as you read this book, it's helpful to keep this in mind.

However, ADHD still impacts both partners and therefore both partners must take steps to optimize their treatment and openly discuss the issues their ADHD can create. Here's Nancie's take on dual-ADHD couples:

"Both my husband and I have ADHD, with mine at a somewhat more moderate level than Steve's. This can create an interesting dynamic. We can empathize quite a bit with both sides of the ADHD/non-ADHD equation. And it is important that we do our best to remember that it is often not the person but the symptoms that are at play when issues arise.

However, there are times when I'm not as caring or sensitive as I could be when pointing out an ADHD behavior that is troubling me. There are also times when my ADHD presents in unappealing ways.. And during hours of the day when medication has worn off, such as in the evening, we both need to be very conscientious to not let little irritations turn into bigger problems.

A profound example of how we are both ADHD, yet very different, involves our evening schedules. Steve's energy slumps around dinnertime, and he mindfully takes a rest to recharge himself. Then, when he wakes up from his rest, he suddenly has lots of energy and can almost perform another day's work into the wee hours of the morning. I, on the other hand, often work at my office until 7-8 p.m., and when I get home, it's wind-down time. By 11, being sensitive to sensory stimulation (a characteristic of some ADHDers), I want all conversation to end, and a quiet to settle over my environment. Our diverse patterns used to create much conflict. He wanted to talk, I wanted to veg. And he'd take offense to me breaking off communication. I would get angry that he couldn't understand my needs. It went on this way until we became better educated about the course our different symptoms were taking. Once we both reached a better understanding of what we were dealing with, our interactions improved. We realized we needed to be more compassionate with one another instead of taking each other's habits as a sign that we didn't care.

I really empathize with ADHD/other ADHD couples. It's like you've been hit with a double whammy. And yet, there are so many blessings that can come from this combination. Steve and I have found opportunities to put our creative energies together, to serve in our community together, to bounce ideas off each other, to have fun together. The opportunities are endless.

Kudos to all readers with ADHD who are reading this book, and particularly to those in dual ADHD relationships who must both tackle ADHD. It takes love and perseverance to resolve the issues that may come up, but you can prevail!"

Diagnosis, Treatment and the Two of You

"Lacking self-control robs you of free will. This is one of the most tragic consequences of ADHD. You might think that you're doing what you desire. Yet if you can't inhibit your behavior, you miss out on the delay between an event and your response. That delay is essential: It gives you the chance to think. Even more critically, that delay empowers you to choose freely."

—Russell Barkley

Treatment is one of the first things couples think about when they discover one or both of them has ADHD. But managing ADHD is complex, as there is no one-size-fits-all treatment. Because of this complexity, our information about treatment can be found in two different places. This chapter provides a concise overview of what we think you need to know about optimizing treatment of ADHD. With this knowledge you can move on to the good stuff—creating a happy relationship.

Our second resource is the ***Overview of Treatments for Adult ADHD*** on Melissa's website (www.adhdmarriage.com). This site provides more in-depth information about specific treatment options and issues. Moreover, it is updated regularly and includes numerous links to important online information.

Because we are not medical doctors, Dr. Edward Hallowell and Dr. John Ratey graciously agreed to review and approve this chapter. They are practicing psychiatrists and co-authors of *Driven to Distraction* and many other books on ADHD. Hallowell and Ratey are two of the world's leading medical experts on ADHD.

HOTSPOT 1
Confusion about Diagnosis and Treatment

With no proven physiological tests for ADHD at this time, getting the right diagnosis is something of an art form. Clinicians must assess:

- Whether or not the cluster of symptoms and behaviors clearly indicate ADHD
- Whether these symptoms might be something else (such as bipolar disorder) that looks similar to ADHD
- If ADHD (if it exists) is complicated by coexisting conditions, such as anxiety, depression or sleep disorders

Diagnosis is just the very beginning of what is typically a longer-than-expected journey on the way to creating a thriving relationship. As this journey unfolds, it is typical that non-ADHD partners suffer from anxieties and pose questions related to the repetitive nature of entrenched ADHD symptoms. For example, while observing their partner's slow progress at managing ADHD symptoms, they might wonder, *Is my partner really dedicated to this? If so, why isn't he working harder to address his ADHD?* As understandable as these feelings and uncertainties are, they miss the larger point. People with ADHD have trouble getting organized and following through. That's part of having ADHD. Since, by definition, those with ADHD have trouble getting organized, it is a cart-before-the-horse challenge for them to be organized enough to get a diagnosis and then put effective treatment in place. The process can be frustrating for both partners—particularly early on.

But let's start at the beginning—with the diagnosis. If you wish to skip to treatment information, go to page 18.

> **ADHD partner:** *I've just found out that I probably have ADHD. Figuring out what to do next just seems completely overwhelming. Can you give me some ideas of where to start?*

> **ADHD partner:** *Are there physical tests I can take instead of having a psychological evaluation? I'm 55 and may have trouble recalling childhood memories. I may also have a hard time coming up with specific examples that help me answer the questions.*

A psychiatrist, psychologist or primary care physician familiar with ADHD is your best resource for an ADHD diagnosis. In some areas you'll find the local expert is a pediatric psychiatrist, whom you may wish to contact. Expertise with ADHD is what you should seek, as ADHD can be tricky to diagnose accurately because it often is accompanied by other conditions such as anxiety or depression that can obscure it. In addition, other conditions such as sleep apnea, bipolar disorder, undiagnosed celiac disease, or a very hectic and overscheduled life can superficially mimic ADHD. Ask your doctor how often she diagnoses and treats ADHD to make sure she will be good at teasing apart the various diagnostic options.

If your current physicians don't have the expertise to diagnose ADHD, there are some other resources available to find help. These include:

- **CHADD** (Children and Adults with Attention Deficit Disorder), a national organization that keeps a small online database of professionals in the field of ADHD.

In addition, and often a better bet, local CHADD chapters may keep a list of local resources. Contact the chapter nearest you to see if it has such a list.

- **The short but growing referrals list** at www.adhdmarriage.com.
- **The PsychologyToday.com online database.** This site is large and allows you to search by zip code and insurance plan. Make sure to call and ask if the person you find genuinely has expertise in ADHD. Many in this database have checked the "treats ADHD" box along with a long list of other options, suggesting they are not specialists in ADHD.
- **Your local school district or learning disabilities group**, which often knows of professionals in your area.
- **A Google search** of "ADHD diagnosis in (your state or city)" or "ADHD doctors in (your state or city)." The search may help you find resources worth exploring. For the sake of evaluation, avoid any resources you find that tout "alternative approaches" or that aren't licensed. You can assess these alternative resources for treatment later, once you know whether or not you have ADHD.
- **The online database at GoodTherapy.org**. Although the "expert search" is somewhat hidden, this site does provide useful information. At the time of this printing, you must go to www.goodtherapy.org then choose "find a therapist," then the "advanced search" tab. Finally, click on "concerns" and choose "Inattention, Impulsivity & Hyperactivity: (ADHD)." To refine your search, choose a state before clicking "search."
- **ADHD-specific clinics**. Some major medical centers, such as Massachusetts General Hospital in Boston and Mt. Sinai Medical Center in New York City, have these. Check your local hospital.

- **Clinics that specialize in Cognitive Behavioral Therapy**. These clinics may also know of local diagnosticians.

A good diagnosis will include a look at your personal and family history, your medical issues and, possibly, your marital concerns. You will be asked questions to understand whether or not you qualify for a diagnosis as established in the diagnostic manual (known as the DSM-5).

Your doctor may also use a computer program to test the speed of your responses and your ability to stay focused on a task. Separately, in 2013, the FDA approved the use of an EEG to aid in ADHD diagnoses when used in conjunction with a full diagnostic interview and testing. This ruling is considered controversial by many, as it is based on a single study of 275 children done by the manufacturer of the EEG machine.

Some doctors (particularly those who don't specialize in ADHD) may give you a quick diagnosis after a brief review of your concerns and a discussion of your history. If you've done your research and you're pretty convinced that you have garden-variety ADHD, this may suffice, though it's not ideal because of all the possible coexisting conditions. However, diagnosis should never be based solely on whether or not you respond to stimulant medication. This is an inappropriate and dangerous form of diagnosis, as you will likely gain more focus using a stimulant whether or not you have ADHD. A hasty diagnosis could lead to an incorrect conclusion or a diagnosis that overlooks other important conditions (such as depression, anxiety, or sleep deprivation) that often go hand in hand with ADHD.

If you can, ask for handouts about ADHD and any treatments you discuss with your doctor. It's hard to remember all of the information he or she will give you.

Is It ADHD or ADD, and Is It Mild or Severe?

> ***Non-ADHD partner:*** *Is there a difference between ADHD and ADD? When I think of ADHD I think of the classic person who can't sit still. Yet my ADD partner seems to have no energy and is often in la la land.*

> ***ADHD partner:*** *Is it possible to have "mild" ADD, and how might this affect my relationship?*

First, "attention deficit hyperactivity disorder" is misnamed. ADHD isn't about a *deficit* of attention—it's about attention *dysregulation*. A person with ADHD can be very distractible much of the time but also have periods of intense focus, sometimes called *hyperfocus*. The "deficit" is really a deficit of control, or regulation, over one's attention. Just because a person with ADHD *wants* to pay attention to something doesn't mean he or she will be *able* to do so at that moment. ADHD treatment is all about putting strategies in place to help the person with ADHD have more control over his or her attention, emotional regulation, memory and behaviors.

ADHD can vary greatly in intensity. Those with milder ADHD might find they are somewhat distractible and not at all impulsive, while others are so distractible they can barely function and are also wildly impulsive, highly emotionally reactive, terrible organizers of projects and time, and have very poor short-term memory. It's not surprising that there is a correlation between the severity of ADHD symptoms and a person's ability/inability to succeed in a wide variety of life functions such as work, dating, schooling and driving.

In addition to different levels of intensity, there are also different types of ADHD. Distraction is the primary symptom of the condition that used to be called ADD (but is now just included in ADHD) whereas hyperactivity (alone or in combination with distraction) is a symptom of other subtypes of ADHD. So ADHD looks very different in different people.

What Else Might it Be?

ADHD partner: *In the diagnostic process, what are the disorders most likely to be confused with ADHD?*

ADHD partner: *My doctor has diagnosed me with both ADHD and anxiety. Is there any rule about what should be treated first?*

In a review of the research about ADHD in adults, researchers and ADHD experts Russell Barkley, Ph.D., Kevin Murphy, Ph.D., and Mariellen Fischer, Ph.D., found that more than 80% of adults with ADHD will experience at least one other condition in their lifetime, more than 50% will experience two or more, and more than one-third will experience three or more conditions[1] (Barkley, Murphy & Fischer, 2008, p. 241).

The most common conditions that coexist with ADHD are listed below. The incidence percentages are in ranges (from multiple research studies) that give you an idea of the likelihood of co-occurrence:

- **Depression:** 16-31% may be currently depressed, with a lifetime likelihood of 53%.
- **Anxiety:** 24-43% of those with ADHD may also suffer from anxiety, depending upon a number of factors.
- **Oppositional Defiant Disorder:** 24-35% of those with ADHD may also be diagnosed with ODD, a disorder characterized by being overly stubborn or rebellious, and refusing to obey rules.
- **Conduct Disorder:** 17-25% of adults with ADHD may also have this. Those with CD often lie, cheat, steal, fight or bully others.

1. For a detailed overview of coexisting conditions, see *ADHD in Adults: What the Science Says* by Russell A. Barkley, Kevin R. Murphy, and Mariellen Fischer, The Guildford Press, 2008, pp. 205-244. See pp. 291-304 for information about drug use and substance abuse. Except where noted, coexisting conditions statistics come from this resource.

- **Dyslexia and Dyscalculia:** Considered a reading disability, dyslexia shows up in at least 20% of individuals with ADHD, according to Dr. Ned Hallowell. (Hallowell & Ratey, n.d.). Dyscalculia (a learning disability related to calculations) and dysgraphia (visual processing) also occur with greater frequency in those who have ADHD than the general population.
- **Alcohol Dependence or Substance Abuse:** People with ADHD can have addictive tendencies, perhaps due to low impulse control or chemical issues in the brain. The likelihood that someone with ADHD will have an alcohol abuse issue in his or her lifetime is 21-53%. Those with ADHD are also more likely to use other substances, particularly marijuana and psychedelics. Interestingly, some research done with young adults found that the correlation between ADHD and substance abuse may be directly tied to the combination of having *both* ADHD and co-occurring conduct disorder.
- **Tobacco Use:** Repeated studies indicate that there is a direct correlation between the number and severity of ADHD symptoms and the use of tobacco. This may be because nicotine has a stimulant-like effect similar to the ADHD medication methylphenidate—in other words, nicotine is a form of self-medication for ADHD. About 40% of adults with ADHD smoke ("Smoking and ADHD: What," n.d.).
- **Other co-existing conditions:** Tourette syndrome (very rare, but with some overlap with ADHD); learning disabilities (very common); bipolar disorder (research varies about whether there is an increased incidence of bipolar in those who also have ADHD); sleep apnea. Fifteen percent of those with ADHD have celiac disease (Niederhofer, n.d.).

What to Treat First

Knowing what else you may have along with ADHD will help your doctor provide the best treatment. If you have a history of depression, for example, your doctor might choose to start treating both the ADHD and your depression with an anti-depressant rather than a stimulant medication. If you don't have a long-term history of depression, on the other hand, it might be valuable to treat the ADHD symptoms first, as depression or anxiety might be tied to the untreated ADHD. Once the ADHD is discovered and treated, the other conditions might disappear.

According to Dr. John Ratey, co-occurring anxiety is often treated successfully with ADHD medication, so the two issues can be handled simultaneously. As he says, "The evolutionary reason for this [i.e., the link between anxiety and ADHD] is that we need to be anxious when we are not focused. As we become more focused we get less anxious. Though this seems paradoxical to many, it is nevertheless true." (J. Ratey, personal communication, December 2, 2013.)

Misdiagnosis

Some disorders look a lot like ADHD but aren't. These include sleep deprivation, sleep apnea, an eye tracking disorder, and something that Hallowell calls "pseudo ADD." The latter may occur when your life is overfilled with commitments and your brain becomes overwhelmed. To rule out the possibility of pseudo ADD, eliminate some of your commitments. If your distraction and feelings of being overwhelmed go away, you don't have ADHD.

Bipolar disorder is often confused with ADHD (and sometimes coexists with it). Bipolar disorder is a mood disorder, and those who have it suffer from extended rages, long periods of sleep deprivation, manic behavior, racing thoughts and more.

Multi-Modal Treatment for ADHD–A Stool with Three Legs

You most likely have ADHD either because you inherited it or because of a brain trauma. As there are many genes involved in the expression of ADHD, it is not completely understood yet. Most of these genes are associated with the neurotransmitters dopamine and norepinephrine, chemicals that are important to the attention and reward systems of the brain. So this means that ADHD is about the chemistry of your brain. But that's not all. It is also about the developmental rate, size and functionality of specific areas of the brain.[2]

Though not all of the details are well understood, the net result is difficulty in the attention and reward systems of the brain, as well as in what are called "executive functions."

What's most important is to understand how to optimize treatment so that ADHD symptoms are managed well enough to get out of the way of a thriving relationship. To help our clients optimize treatment, we describe it as having three legs, like a stool. And, like that stool, the best treatment only "stands" if all three legs are employed. You should be consciously selecting options from all three legs. If you are not doing so, you are not optimizing your ability to manage your ADHD. We will describe each leg in more detail later in this chapter.

2. According to Iliyan Ivanov, M.D., of the Mt. Sinai School of Medicine in New York City, brain scans show that those with ADHD tend to have a smaller thalamic surface and that portions of the corpus callosum section of their brain are smaller. In addition, Dr. Hallowell notes that the prefrontal cortex and the vermis of the cerebellum are areas of the brain that "are ever so slightly different" in those who have ADHD. Dr. Martin Teicher, Director of the Developmental Biopsychiatry Research Program of McLean Hospital, observes that there are differences in the cerebellum that show up on MRIs.

What Are Executive Functions (EF)?

Executive functions help you exhibit control over your actions so you can reach a goal you wish to achieve. According to Ari Tuckman (2012), those with ADHD exhibit weaknesses in some or all of these areas:

Working memory:
The ability to hold information in the very short term to use to process two or more things, or until deciding to move the thought to long-term memory. Weak working memory leads to easy distraction, difficulty staying on task, impulsive decision making, forgetfulness, and lack of interest in reading.

Sense of time:
The ability to estimate and monitor the passage of time.

Response inhibition:
The ability to put on the brakes and think before we act. It is also important in delaying gratification.

Prospective memory:
The ability to carry an intention or thought forward in time so you may act on it.

Emotional self-control:
The ability to create perspective that help us keep difficult emotions in check.

Self-activation:
Being able to motivate yourself to do something, even if it's boring or hard.

Hindsight and forethought:
Using lessons from the past to inform current behavior and decisions; the ability to visualize the future to plan a sequence of events.

Target Symptoms

In order to understand how you are doing, it is important to take a baseline before you start treatment if you can. Use a symptom tracking worksheet like the one we will describe in a moment, and add these items:

- Weight and regularity of meals
- Sleep patterns: when you typically sleep, and for how long
- Agitation, anger, irritability and emotionality. Are your moods stable? Are there times of the day when you are more likely to be upset or moody (for example, at the end of the day)? Do you explode suddenly in anger and frustration?
- Health issues
- Your ADHD symptoms

Include your partner when making your observations, and write it all down.

You will also want to decide what you will consider "success." The best way to do this is to create a *short* list of target symptoms. With your partner, determine which symptoms most interfere with your life and relationship. Common target symptoms include the following:

- **Distraction**—doesn't pay attention to partner; loses track of things, conversations or tasks
- **Impulsivity**—doesn't think before acting; can't stop anger escalation even when wants to; makes many poor decisions, including financially
- **Poor organization**—can't figure out how to organize or what steps to take when organizing
- **Poor memory**—short-term memory is difficult

- **Initiation/disengagement issues**—procrastinates a lot or, conversely, can't stop whatever he or she is doing… or both
- **Time management**—often late; poor judge of how long something will take; doesn't learn this from experience
- **Anger management**—outbursts; quick emotionality
- **Overwhelms easily**—shuts down quickly in the face of too much emotion or information
- **Sleep problems**—not enough sleep; can't get to bed early enough; sleep apnea; insomnia

You should talk with your doctor about your target symptoms, as they will help her choose the right treatments for you.

The Symptom Reduction Benchmark and Symptom Tracking

Research suggests that significant behavioral change comes when symptom reduction is measured at, or greater than, 50% (Mason, n.d). So that should be your minimum symptom reduction target.

To track shifts in symptom expression, fill out a symptom tracking worksheet either before each visit to your doctor or monthly if your doctor visits are infrequent. One that is often used for adults is the *Adult ADHD Self-Report Scale (ASRS v1.1)*. This can be found in PDF format in the treatment guide at www.adhdmarriage.com. Tracking your symptoms helps you see how you are doing and helps you remember to keep it up.

It's a great idea to have both spouses track symptoms. It is fairly common for someone with ADHD to be unaware of symptomatic behaviors that are having a big impact on a partner. So it's good to get that partner's input.

Leg 1: Physiological Treatments

Since ADHD is about brain chemistry and function, Leg 1 treatments are all about balancing out that chemistry and function. In other words, they involve changing the way your brain works. This leg includes medication as well as other non-medicinal treatments. The best of the "other" treatments include improved sleep, exercise, and adding Omega 3s to your diet. All Leg 1 treatments create a new balance in the chemistry of your brain, thus optimizing function and helping you manage symptoms.

The results of using treatments from Leg 1 can be impressive. Research suggests that medication can "normalize" (we hate that word, but it gets the idea across…) behavior for 50-65% of adults with ADHD and offer significant relief to another 20-30% of adults (Barkley & Benton, 2010, p. 16). Those are impressive numbers—and that's just medication. Adding sleep improvements and exercise can help you do even better. The bottom line is that for the vast majority of you, there is a treatment that can help.

Leg 1 treatments can enhance focus, diminish hyperactivity of the mind or body, clear your mind, and more. That's amazing, but what's important from a *relationship* perspective is what you *do* with that new clarity and attention. You must take your ability to focus better and then apply that focus to improving the behaviors you exhibit with your partner. *That's* where the rubber meets the road for your relationship. Improved focus remains in your head—completely unavailable to anyone else but you—until you do something with that focus to change how you act in the world. So when you think about treatment, don't think about the Leg 1 treatments such as medication as the "end" of treatment. Consider them a beginning. Medication and other Leg 1 treatments are simply tools you can use to live your life more easily and support the focus needed to learn to interact with your partner and family more reliably and happily.

What follows is an overview. It is *not* intended to be a complete listing of medications, their side effects, contraindications or warnings. Please make sure to fully discuss any medication with your doctor to determine if it is right for you.

Stimulant Medications

Medications alter the brain's ability to produce or retain certain chemicals, thus improving brain function. Stimulants are often the first type of medication tried, in part because doctors and patients can see the results of taking them quickly. In addition, stimulants have been used for decades, have been heavily researched, and are considered safe to use when used properly.

There are two main families of stimulants: the methylphenidates and the amphetamines. The **methylphenidates** include brand names such as Concerta, Metadate, Ritalin, Daytrana Patch, Methylin, Focalin, Quillivant and Biphentin (in Canada).

The **amphetamine** family includes brand names such as Adderall, Vyvanse and Dexedrine. Methylphenidate and amphetamine both act by inhibiting the reuptake of dopamine and norepinephrine. In addition, amphetamine facilitates the release of dopamine. Amphetamines, unlike the methylphenidates, are sensitive to how much vitamin C is in your system—the more vitamin C, the faster it clears from your body. In addition, *misuse* of amphetamines can cause very serious issues, including death.

There are different release variations for stimulants—immediate release, intermediate and once-daily preparations. And each specific medication has its own profile—released once, twice, thrice, or consistently across the span of time the medication stays in your body. Specifics on this topic are online in the treatment overview.

Unfortunately, with so many choices, there isn't any set pattern for what stimulant medication will work for whom. Some people respond to one variety of stimulant, some to another. Some get side effects from one and not others. If you have co-existing conditions, such as depression, you may also need a second medication.

We don't tell you about the complexity to scare you. Rather, we want you to have realistic expectations. You and your doctor will need to experiment with a number of different options to find the one that works best for you, and it will likely take some time to get it right.

Other Medications

There are other, non-stimulant, medications used to treat ADHD. The following medication descriptions have been modified from information contained in Hallowell and Ratey's book on adult ADHD, *Delivered from Distraction*.

Atomoxetine (brand name Strattera) is an often-prescribed non-stimulant ADHD medication that primarily blocks norepinephrine reuptake in the brain. It does not target dopamine (though it may raise dopamine in some specific areas of the brain). Therefore it works better than stimulants for some people and worse for others. It may also be a particularly good choice for those who are worried about addiction issues, as it does not impact the reward centers of the brain associated with addiction. It is considered to have no abuse potential and can be stopped, if necessary, with no ill effects. The full effects of Strattera can take 2-4 weeks to become apparent.

Bupropion (brand names Wellbutrin, Zyban) is another effective treatment for adult ADHD that works by increasing norepinephrine and altering dopamine levels in the brain. It is not approved by the FDA for ADHD treatment but is regularly used off label for that purpose. It has the advantage of providing 24-hour coverage and not elevating heart rate or blood pressure.

Modafinil (brand names NuVigil, Provigil) is usually used in combination with other medications. It makes you alert without providing the "push" or urgent feelings that stimulants sometimes provide and tends to improve time management, prioritization skills and the like. It also helps smooth out the ups and downs of stimulant medications.

Alpha Agonists (brand names Kapvay, Intuniv, Clonidine, Tenex) were introduced to lower blood pressure. They are used to help reduce hyperactivity in the mind and to induce sleep. They can also be used to treat aggression and regulate moods. However, these drugs are powerful and can cause significant issues when used in conjunction with other medications. Several cases of sudden death were reported when Clonidine was used in conjunction with Ritalin, so please avoid that combination.

Beta Blockers may be used by some physicians in combination with either stimulants or antidepressants to treat impulsivity, tantrums, feelings of inner tenseness, anger and anxiety.

Tricyclics, which are older anti-depressants, are also sometimes used because they impact norepinephrine levels. However, they can have significant side effects (including death) and are really a last line option treatment.

Your doctor can discuss your options for the best treatment for your specific target symptoms, co-occurring conditions, and physical health.

Medication Dosing and Measurement of Response

If you are taking a stimulant, your dose is at least as important as the brand and type of stimulant you are taking. Again, there is a wide range of doses people of similar size might take. Some are highly sensitive to the medications, while others are not sensitive at all. As a result, physicians will usually start with a small dose of one type of stimulant, then work to larger doses and/or a different stimulant altogether based upon your response. Higher doses do more to address core symptoms than lower doses…until you get to the point where the dose is too high. Too high a dose of a methylphenidate, for example, may make you feel "stoned" or zombie-like. Too much of an amphetamine may increase anger, irritability and tension.

So start low, and work your way up until you obtain symptom relief without difficult side effects. If you have side effects, talk with your doctor about lowering the dose again, adding a second medication at a very low dose, or trying a different medication altogether.

Though it takes time to experiment to find just the right dose and medication (often many months), it is well worth the effort. In research, the impact a medication has on target symptoms is measured in "effect size." The greater the effect size, the better the result. The benchmark for a solid, robust effect size is a 1.0. The effect size for stimulants in blind clinical trials is .95—in other words, quite good. The effect size for stimulants in optimized dose trials where patients worked with doctors to take just the right dose was 2.2! That's a big difference, and means you should keep working with your doctor until you feel comfortable that you are getting the best you can from your medications. There is more on the effect size of various treatments in the online treatment guide.

Medication Coverage

The ideal ADHD medication is one that works well for you and provides symptom relief all of the time you are awake. Wellbutrin and Strattera have the potential for 24-hour coverage, and Vyvanse mimics full coverage for some. To get good, 12-16 hour coverage with some of the stimulants, you may have to take medications multiple times during the day. Your doctor can help you create a schedule to do this.

> **Non-ADHD partner:** *My spouse takes medication for work and seems to be improving in that realm. But by the time he's home, the meds have worn off. Plus, he says he likes to take a break from the meds on the weekends. This strikes me as unfair!*

If you have ADHD and are interested in improving your relationship, then taking medications at home as well as at work makes sense. This woman is right—if ADHD symptoms are a problem, then taking a break on weekends is not a great approach to creating a happy relationship. If your desire to take a break stems from side effects, then talk with your doctor about your treatment options.

Medication Side Effects

Medications for ADHD are generally well tolerated, and side effects, if they do occur, are often mild and can usually be addressed through changing dosage or medication.

There are a few side effects that we want to make you aware of. *Please make sure to talk with your doctor about the side effects of the specific medication you are considering taking and any interactions they might have with other medications you take. In most cases you can take medication with very few or no side effects and still see much improvement in target symptoms.*

What we've listed here is not a complete list!

- **Interferes with sleep:** If you are taking a stimulant medication that interferes with your sleep, you may be negating the benefits of the medication—perhaps completely—because sleep deprivation increases ADHD symptoms. Take your final dose earlier in the day, take a lower dose, or consider a different medication altogether.
- **Appetite suppression:** According to Dr. Hallowell, appetite suppression is by far the most common side effect of stimulants. See your doctor if unwanted weight loss occurs.
- **Anger/irritability:** Stimulants can increase irritability or anger. If this happens to you, try a different dose or different medication. Anger and irritability are not good side effects in a relationship!
- **Suicidal thinking:** A very rare but known side effect of Strattera is suicidal thinking. If you decide to try Strattera, make sure that both you and your spouse are alert to changes in your mood. These changes can come on suddenly, so if you start to feel depressed or suicidal, assume it is the medication and *immediately* seek help.

Non-Medicinal Leg 1 Treatments

Exercise

It's not news that exercising is good for you. From the perspective of treating ADHD, exercise has very specific benefits. *Aerobic* exercise can alter brain chemistry (temporarily) and function (long-term) to:

- Create a period of a couple of hours of improved focus immediately after physical activity. Exercising right before you need a boost of attention can be used strategically to boost attention for meetings, time with family, and taking on things that are particularly difficult
- Over time create new neural pathways that improve learning, retention, attention, and more through a process called neurogenesis
- Significantly diminish depression and anxiety, which often accompany ADHD
- Improve mood in general, helping you stay calm in spousal interactions
- Enhance cognitive function

According to Dr. John Ratey, an expert on the impact of exercise on the brain, you want to get at least 30 minutes of moderate to intense exercise every day. To do so, try brisk walking, running, riding a bike, jumping rope, swimming, or… you name it. Just try to get your heart rate up enough so that you are sweating. If you can get more than those 30 minutes, great!

You can also use brief spurts of exercise to reboot your brain when you start to fade. Say you are sitting at your computer too long. Just stand up and do 25 jumping jacks, or jog in place, lifting your knees as high as you can. This will send oxygen flowing to your brain and help energize you for your next session of concentration.

If you find you are having trouble sticking to an exercise routine, consider joining a scheduled class or getting an exercise buddy with whom you commit to specific times to exercise.

Take a Brain Break!

Dr. John Ratey suggests that 3-5 minutes of fairly intense exercise is great preparation for work that requires you to concentrate fully—like homework, presentations for work, or listening to your mate. Walk or run up stairs, jump rope, run in place, or do jumping jacks to get your heart rate up. It really turns on the executive functions!

Sleep

We cannot emphasize enough how important good sleep is to those who have ADHD. We also know how hard it is for many with ADHD to get it.

Study after study reports that adults need approximately 8 hours of sleep a night to function at peak cognition. As an added perk, 8 hours of sleep a night forestalls cognitive decline, Alzheimer's, and diabetes. It also helps you keep weight off! Even *30 minutes* less than 8 hours a night has a measurable negative effect on your ability to think and work. People who have survived on less sleep than that for decades often think that they don't need as much sleep as everyone else. Nope. A very, very small proportion of the population needs less sleep than 8 hours—we're talking perhaps 3%.[3] Chances are, that's *not* you! This means it's VERY likely you BOTH need more sleep.

Sleep deprivation significantly increases the expression of ADHD symptoms and decreases your ability to manage your emotions. Let's turn that around: the reason it's important for you to take your sleep schedule *really* seriously is that sleep is

3. See the work of Dr. Daniel Buyesse, University of Pittsburgh, on "short sleepers."

one of the best treatments around for ADHD. This makes sense. If you already have trouble focusing because of ADHD, the cognitive decline caused by sleep deprivation will just make your focus worse. We've included information about ways to improve your ability to sleep (called "sleep hygiene") in the online treatment overview.

Finally, you should be aware that there is a higher incidence of sleep apnea amongst those who have ADHD. In fact, there is some discussion as to whether or not sleep apnea issues are actually being misdiagnosed as ADHD. In any event, if the sleep hygiene suggestions in the *Overview of Treatments for Adult ADHD* don't work for you, we recommend you consult a sleep specialist to find out if something other than ADHD is going on.

Sleep Tip

Don't watch electronics near bedtime. Unless you use f.lux or a similar app on your computer, the blue light electronics emit "tells" your brain it's time to be awake and diminishes the production of melatonin needed to fall sleep.

Fish Oil and Omega 3s

Our brain needs Omega 3s to function properly, yet the North American diet does not contain enough food rich in this nutrient. As a result, most of us have too much Omega 6 (found in Safflower Oil, Vegetable Oils and many nuts) and too little Omega 3 (found in oily fishes, flax seeds, walnuts and winter squash).

Some research done with children suggests that adding 3,000 mg of fish oil to the diet had an effect size of .59. Incrementally, that's helpful, though it's probably not enough of an impact to suffice as a solo treatment for most. Other research links high doses of fish oil to a decreased risk of inflammatory diseases and heart disease. However, high doses of fish oil may also be associated with an increased risk of prostate cancer. Since the research is mixed, and because there are some contraindications for fish oil, you should talk with your doctor about whether or not fish oil is a good fit for you. There are other ways to get Omega 3s, such as beans and extra virgin olive oil. However, there is no research on these to determine their effectiveness for treating ADHD. As a result of all of this, Dr. Hallowell currently recommends that adults take up to 2,000mg a day of fish oil to help treat ADHD symptoms. Look for fish oil that has higher concentrations of EPA to DHA as studies show them to be better for mood and attentional control.

Nutrition

Meta-analysis of the research done to date on the impact of diet on ADHD symptoms suggests that diet and food additives have a very small impact on ADHD symptoms (Barkley, 2012). The only exceptions were food coloring, which should be eliminated from the diets of those sensitive to food coloring, and fatty acids such as fish oil (Sonuga-Barke et al., 2013).

However, since improving your diet is always good for your health, it probably makes sense to consider trying a shift to see whether a change in diet helps you...particularly if your diet is heavy in sugars and caffeine that might interfere with sleep.

Dr. Hallowell's advice for nutrition changes include the following:

- Eat protein at every meal—this helps keep your energy levels more stable
- Eat primarily vegetables, beans, and whole (rather than processed) grains
- Eliminate sugar and caffeine whenever possible

In other words, do all the things that the nutrition experts suggest.

There is also some evidence that a gluten free diet may substantially improve ADHD symptoms *for those who have undiagnosed celiac disease,* which is more highly represented in the ADHD population than the population at large. Fifteen percent of those with ADHD have celiac disease versus one percent of the general population (Niederhofer, H., n.d.). The data is less clear for those who simply have gluten intolerance. As three data points, Dr. Ned Hallowell (who has ADHD himself) went gluten free for a year and reported a very significant improvement in his symptoms. Dr. John Ratey (who also has ADHD) went grain free and reported more energy, less impulsivity and better motivation. The Orlovs also saw minor improvements in symptoms. All lost weight at the same time. As a data set of three, that's hearsay, not science. On the other hand, it won't hurt you to try it, and if you do see the kind of response that Hallowell and Ratey have seen, you will be thankful. Just remember that you may have to try a gluten free diet for several months before reaching any conclusions. Some suggestions for good GF cookbooks can be found in the online treatment overview.

Self-Medication

A number of habits that ADHD people adopt are actually forms of self-medication. We wish to make you aware of a few but leave it to you to decide whether these forms of self-medication are positive or negative in your relationship:

- **Caffeine**, which is a stimulant and therefore can help provide focus. Too much, though, can interfere with sleep, which then makes symptoms worse. According to Dr. Ratey, energy drinks are particularly dangerous. They work, but at a cost to overall health and are much more dangerous than taking stimulants, as people often don't think of them as medication and therefore use them in erratic, out-of-control ways.
- **Video games:** When you play video games or watch fast-changing films or commercials, your brain responds with little squirts of dopamine. This feels good, though too much time on computers and videos can interfere with connecting with family members.

- **Marijuana:** For some, pot calms an overactive mind. Unfortunately, impulse control issues for those with ADHD can result in using too much pot and hurting other parts of your life, such as your ability to hold a job.
- **Tobacco:** Repeated studies show a correlation between tobacco use and severity of ADHD, possibly because tobacco is a stimulant and therefore used as a form of self-medication.
- **Porn:** Some use porn to quench a chemical "itch" when they feel the need for stimulation. If a partner objects to the porn, impulse control issues can create unwanted conflict.
- **High stimulation activities:** From sky diving to picking fights, highly stimulating activities can feel good to those with ADHD.
- **Sports:** All exercise is good for calming the ADHD mind.

Leg 2: Behavioral and Habit Changes

Leg 1 treatments are all about getting your body and brain into good shape for optimal performance. Leg 2 treatments are about using that improved brainpower and self-control to change your ADHD behavior and habits in ways that will benefit your life.

An easy way to think about this leg is to realize that those with ADHD often need *external structures* to organize their thinking and time. It isn't that people with ADHD don't know what they ought to be doing—it's that they often can't follow through on what they want to do at the right time because symptoms, such as distraction, difficulty planning, and poor short-term memory, interfere. Leg 2 treatments provide the infrastructure so that symptoms like these don't rule—you do. Want to get the car serviced? Use Leg 2 support structures to put it on the calendar and set one or more reminders. Odds are, the car will get serviced.

ADHD adults often suffer from thinking things such as *everybody else seems to be able to do what they say they will. I ought to be able to, as well, if I just try harder.* This is a trap you don't want to fall into! It's not about trying *harder*—it's about trying *differently*. Simplifying and organizing boring tasks comes more easily to non-ADHD partners because the reminder and reward system is there—invisibly—on the *inside* of their heads. For those with ADHD, that internal system is not there—by definition. That's the "executive function problems" description of ADHD. This means you must add external structures that non-ADHD partners don't use.

When those with ADHD *accept* that their reminder system needs to be *external* because of their ADHD—and stop beating themselves up about being different—their lives can get much, much easier. It's just fine that a doctor with ADHD has trouble remembering to put his socks in the hamper with the system he currently uses. It's probably a system that is better suited to someone without ADHD. He might prefer a separate hamper located next to where he gets dressed so that it's within view at the right time. Or he might hang a note next to his bathroom mirror to remind himself to pick up the bedroom right before bed. Taking these steps will ensure that the socks get picked up as well as the pants. Of course, he might have to experiment with different solutions before finding something that works for him. Not everyone is the same or is helped by the same external structures.

ADHD coaches can be a big help with Leg 2 treatments. A good ADHD coach can point you towards possible solutions that have worked for others with ADHD, shortening the time it takes to find the right ideas for you. He or she can also provide temporary external structures (reminders, charts and the like) to help you create new habits.

So, while Leg 1 treatments can provide focus, clarity and calm, Leg 2 treatments are exciting because they put you back in charge of your life! When you have good external structures in place, you can then decide *whether* or not to do something and *when* to do it. You can remind yourself to engage in your relationship more fully when you *want* to. You can *choose* whether or not to express an angry thought that comes to your head. You can...be you! And typically, the real you looks a lot better, and a lot more reliable, trustworthy and *lovable* than those ADHD symptoms.

Getting those Leg 2 behaviors and reminder structures in place takes work! Often adults with ADHD must build this support structure for the first time ever. But it is worth every ounce of effort because these structures put ADHD symptoms back where they belong—under your control. And once that happens, all those other wonderful characteristics you possess, and interests you have, can shine through again.

Strengths-Based Treatment

As each of you ponders what external structures to use, utilize your strengths. If you are a visual person, notes and whiteboards might work well. If you are an audible learner, perhaps using a voice recorder to capture information and setting audible alarms will help. If you like to write, journaling to work out your feelings could be effective. Further, think about structuring your life and tasks around things you do well. Some of us spent a lot of time in school remediating our weaknesses. But as an adult you don't have any paper exams to complete. Once you get past a very basic level of competence, it's much more effective to strengthen your strengths.

As part of a couple, you don't have to do everything well. Steve is the computer whiz in the Kohlenberger household. Anything computers is his bailiwick. Nancie finds joy in planning social activities with their friends. He leaves those "responsibilities" to her.

Everybody has skills and talents. As you search for these, think broadly. Think about qualities such as empathy, creativity, energy, organization and more. An empathetic and energetic partner might make a great caregiver for children, for example, even if he isn't very organized. Remember to play to your strengths as often as possible and to support your partner in doing the same. This will help you both shine!

Best Resources for Leg 2 Treatments

There are numerous resources for great ideas about how to get more organized, plan better, be on time, and accomplish all the other challenging elements of daily life. We mentioned ADHD coaches as one option. There are also many books, videos, and a growing library of online presentations available. We suggest you delve into the topic and search for those ideas that resonate with you. Then experiment to see what works!

Below are a few books we think are quite good. A more complete list appears in our online treatment guide. These books are concise, informative, well organized and, importantly, very positive. You *can* make these changes, and these authors know this because they've seen so many others triumph.

ADD-Friendly Ways to Organize Your Life by Judith Kolberg & Kathleen Nadeau, Ph.D.—this book is organized into sections, such as *Learning to Prioritize* and *Time Awareness*, that get to the heart of ADHD symptom issues and provide specific, actionable ideas for how to manage these issues.

More Attention, Less Deficit: Success Strategies for Adults with ADHD by Ari Tuckman, PsyD, MBA—This book is by far the longest of those we suggest here, but that's because it's about more than just setting structures in place—it also provides interesting, in-depth information about ADHD, treatment, coping strategies and more. Behavioral strategies are listed throughout the book, with the last chapters dedicated to tactics you can try.

Understand Your Brain, Get More Done: The ADHD Executive Functions Workbook by Ari Tuckman, PsyD, MBA—Each chapter of this hands-on workbook introduces an idea, such as *emotional self-control (i.e., having feelings without acting on them)*. The book then reviews how those with ADHD experience the idea, guides you through the process of figuring out how that idea impacts your own life specifically, and provides ideas about what you might do to improve things. This resource is a useful tool and approach because it's informative but streamlined.

Leg 3: Overview of Interactive Improvements

The final leg of our treatment "stool" involves *interactions with your partner*. The overarching concept of this leg is that there are many ways for the two of you to interact around ADHD symptoms. Some provide a positive boost to your relationship while others are quite negative. We want you to use the positive ones!

The rest of this book contains many, many examples of Leg 3 treatments and ways to improve your interactions, but let us give you some overarching concepts to keep in mind. In general, you are moving in the right direction on Leg 3 if you seek ways to interact that are:

- **Respectful** of each other and of the fact that you do things differently.
- **Kind**. This sounds simplistic, but it's important. High levels of frustration often lead to low levels of kindness. Remember, this is your life partner. He or she deserves your kindness.
- **Positively engaged**. Your temptation, if you are struggling, may be to disengage. It's often easier than negotiating your differences. Unfortunately, disengaging typically increases your problems over the long-term.
- **Honest about your needs**. We never encourage couples to bury their needs, only to express them in a way that is respectful and kind.
- **ADHD aware**. ADHD will remain a part of your relationship. Guard against symptom or motivation misinterpretation. Remind yourselves to seek ADHD-friendly approaches to the issues that come up in your lives.

It's important to reiterate a key point: if your partner thinks that ADHD—or responses to ADHD—are hurting your relationship, then you should respond even if you don't agree. After all, *responding is a form of respect and validation*. There is nothing that says an ADHD partner must take medication. But not choosing *some* form of ADHD treatment and behavior modification is a way of saying *I don't care what you think or what your problems are*. That's not respectful, validating, or kind! Ditto for non-ADHD partners. If your partner suggests you are controlling, angry or some other description you find hard to hear, *don't ignore it!* We urge you BOTH to engage in Leg 3 treatment.

Are You Optimizing Your Treatment?

To see how robust your treatment is, consider using the downloadable *ADHD Effect Treatment Worksheet* found at www.adhdmarriage.com. It will help you see whether there are incremental ways to manage your ADHD symptoms.

Treatment for Non-ADHD Partners

Living with someone with undermanaged or untreated ADHD is stressful, and many non-ADHD partners develop physiological and emotional problems in response. Depression and anxiety are common, as are physical issues related to stress. Non-ADHD partners need to make sure that they don't ignore their own health as they focus on ADHD-related issues. See a doctor or therapist if you feel depressed, anxious or sick. Get plenty of sleep and exercise. Eat right. And make sure you get enough time with friends and family, as well as your partner, so you will continue to have a life you love.

Learning to manage ADHD is a marathon, not a sprint. You need to be physiologically and mentally ready for the long run.

HOTSPOT 2
Resisting Diagnosis or Treatment

Non-ADHD partner: *My husband has ADHD and is currently undiagnosed. He is less concerned about getting diagnosed than I feel he should be, and we are arguing about this quite a bit. What's the best way to approach this problem?*

Non-ADHD partner: *My partner is taking medications for ADHD but is doing nothing else, so not much has changed for us. He doesn't think his ADHD is a very big deal. What do I do?*

Many adults who will eventually be diagnosed with ADHD initially resist the idea that they might have it. When we've talked with adults about this, they tell us they:

- Thought ADHD was only for kids.
- Can't have ADHD because they know someone with ADHD and they are nothing like this person. They don't realize that those with ADHD show symptoms in different ways.
- Thought they were doing fine.
- Resented the idea that their partner might be asking for an evaluation in order to be able to blame them for their relationship troubles.
- Could easily see their partner's anger, frustration, stress or other issues and felt this was the real reason for their troubles.
- Were successful at work and therefore couldn't have ADHD (unfortunately, this is a misconception held by some doctors, too).

- Were tired of their partner's nagging and pressure and didn't want to give in, just on principle.
- Thought that smart people didn't have ADHD (intelligence is not correlated with whether or not you have ADHD).

Even after diagnosis, relationship problems encouraged by ADHD symptoms might continue. Melissa and George fought about whether ADHD mattered for two years after his diagnosis. George angrily summed up his feelings about Melissa's claims that ADHD was a problem by saying, "You are the one who is unhappy in this relationship! You obviously have a problem with me. But I don't have a problem with me—I'm just fine! You're the one with the problem!!!"

If you are asking an ADHD partner to consider diagnosis or treatment and are facing resistance, we urge you to drop the label of ADHD for a while. Focus, instead, on the *issues* that show up in your relationship. Ultimately, it is the issues that need to be addressed. If, at some point in the future, the two of you continue to struggle and are searching for other approaches, then return to the possibility of ADHD. At that point you'll be able to refer to what tactics didn't work and bolster your point of view that considering ADHD might be useful.

The Label of ADHD and Bias

Controversial research from Harvard about the nature of bias indicates that our brain may make associations that lead us to connect certain ideas with certain labels (Levitin, 2013). This isn't just cultural. It is *physiologically* easier for us to make some associations than others. This has implications in your relationship.

ADHD partner: *I hate the idea of being labeled as ADHD.*

Some people resist even the idea of getting an ADHD diagnosis because of its negative associations in the media and among friends. Trying to change how you view ADHD and calling it *a different way of being in the world* can help but doesn't fully address the issue.

It's easy for people to harbor unconscious biases about what the label ADHD means. Typical associations might include the following: incompetent, "needs help," thoughtless, rude, dumb, slow, broken, stubborn and more. These associations may well come more freely than associations such as creative, unique, free-spirited, considering all options, energetic, or independent. As you were reading, which set of words was easier for you to associate with? Did one of them stop you short? Both sets are objectively true, but you may have found it easier to associate ADHD with the first set than the second. ADHD partner wariness of the label "ADHD" has merit.

The best approach that a non-ADHD partner can take when faced with resistance about the importance of ADHD or any leg of treatment is to:

- Acknowledge that the biases against being labeled ADHD are worthy of concern, and work diligently to combat any personal biases. We hope concerns over bias will not stand in the way of an evaluation and diagnosis, for learning to manage ADHD has great value.
- Acknowledge that ADHD is your partner's health issue. Like it or not, it's your partner's body and should be under his or her control—not yours.
- Not dictate either diagnosis or specific types of treatment. Focus instead on the issues that you feel the two of you have in the relationship. You don't care *how* your ADHD partner addresses those issues, only *that* she addresses those issues!
- Take the pressure off. Sometimes resistance is a knee-jerk response to feeling as if a non-ADHD partner is trying to exert too much control.

- Work on your own issues immediately. You probably have them, and it's hard to request your partner make changes when you aren't doing so yourself.

Medication Reminders?

> **Non-ADHD partner:** *My husband often forgets to take his meds but gets upset if I remind him. I don't know what to do. I was so looking forward to some changes for the better. Now his forgetfulness is causing a problem.*

Like it or not, the person who has ADHD is in charge of the body that displays the ADHD behaviors. This leaves non-ADHD or other-ADHD partners in the position of *lobbying* for what they believe should happen, without taking over responsibility for the partner's actions by parenting or nagging. It's a very fine line between lobbying and demanding, and sometimes it's hard to keep from crossing it. Remembering that you are a supplicant, not a dictator, can help.

Reminding your partner to take medications is parenting behavior and should be avoided. Instead, see if a longer-term pattern of forgetfulness or inconsistency develops, and talk about medication management in general as an important tool in calming your relationship. In that conversation you can reiterate how helpful it is when there is a system in place to ensure medication is taken regularly.

Sometimes a person suspects he / she might have ADHD but can't manage to make the appointment for diagnosis. In this instance, we suggest an open conversation. If the partner with suspected ADHD really does wish to get a diagnosis but just can't remember to pick up the phone or do the necessary research, then we think it's appropriate for the non-ADHD partner to offer to make the appointment. This gets the ball rolling by removing a stumbling block that just doesn't need to be there. Your partner wants to get help, and this is a small contribution to your mutual progress.

In general, our advice is to try to remain a *partner* rather than a *parent figure* in the search for getting ADHD treatment right. Actions appropriate for partners include:

- Offering temporary help if it's needed. However, leave it up to the ADHD partner to decide whether to accept that help. Do NOT take on the role of long-term reminder person. That's for audible alarms or calendars!
- Being a second point of reference for symptom tracking, if the ADHD partner agrees. Two sets of eyes are better than one.
- Making suggestions for reminder structures without dictating their use. For example, you might say, "I saw a great pillbox today that glows bright red if you haven't taken your pill at the right time!"
- Reinforcing positive behavior as it happens with comments, such as "I noticed how focused you were today and it was so great!" or "I'm so delighted you decided to use a coach!"

We urge both partners to remain patient but also committed to forward progress. It often takes a long time—months, not weeks—to get medications figured out, so giving ADHD partners some breathing space is good. Remember to remain respectful of the ADHD partner's efforts to put treatment strategies in place. If it were easy, it would have happened a long time ago.

Tomato/Tomahto– Overcoming Communication Issues

"We are stronger when we listen, and smarter when we share."

— Rania Al-Abdullah

Right now, you may not be happy with the way you interact with your partner. There may be more angry or frustrating conversations than you want, and perhaps you feel as if the other person doesn't "hear" you well enough. You feel you ought to be able to communicate with each other more easily.

Or maybe you communicate well enough when discussing daily chores but still aren't hearing your partner tell you how much he cares.

This chapter will look at how to address communication "hot spots" couples often struggle with when impacted by ADHD. We hope to provide you with many ideas you can use immediately to smooth out your interactions and help you thrive. Make sure to also read the chapter on anger. A better understanding of the way that you interact while angry will help you be more constructive when you communicate your anger.

Improving your communication will take practice. But over time, and with some good new strategies in place, you should be able to accept each other in a loving way, validate your partner's positions and responses, and feel loved, appreciated and heard.

Some Perspective First–Differences Between You Impact Communication

> **ADHD partner:** *I know that my spouse and I are different, but I seem to have a huge problem gauging her response to various things that I may say or do even though I've attempted to think things out to avoid this. Is this typical in an ADHD/non-ADHD relationship? If so, is this a problem we can overcome?*

You already know this, but it's worth saying again: you and your partner are very different! What may be less obvious is how those differences impact your communication. It's worth considering differences in your physiological intake of information as well as in your past experiences.

You Experience Events Differently

Dr. Ned Hallowell likes to say, quite positively, that people with ADHD *inhabit the world differently* than people without ADHD. He also jokes that many of those *without* ADHD have ASD, or Attention Surplus Disorder.

It's true—we do experience things differently. When you are struggling with communication issues, understanding this is critical. When you experience things differently, *you may also interpret them differently* and come to different conclusions. How often have you been surprised at your spouse's interpretation of an event? You might be tempted to say, "That's not what happened!" But before you do, consider this: what your partner is saying is *exactly* what happened—for your partner.

Understanding your differences is important. Here are a few to keep in mind as you strive to improve your communication:

- The ADHD brain is somewhat "unfiltered." Everything enters at about the same level. This means that lots of information is vying for attention, and it's very hard to differentiate and organize. (On the positive side, an abundance of information can nourish creativity.) Conversely, non-ADHD partners may have hierarchical brains that filter out even more than they realize.
- People with ADHD tend to live in the moment. They tend to "go with the flow" and react to their environment. Those without ADHD spend a good amount of time anticipating what will happen next, planning for the future and ruminating about the past. They may more proactively "make things happen."
- Those with ADHD often get from point A to point B in a non-linear fashion. This contrasts with many non-ADHD partners, who pride themselves on their efficiency.
- Many with ADHD have difficulty managing time, controlling impulses, and planning. Such tasks are often strengths for non-ADHD partners.

Neither partner's experience is "right" or "wrong," but they can be *quite* different.

Accepting that neither experience is superior has a lot of advantages, one of which has to do with correctly interpreting memories. We all assume that the way we see and experience the world around us is "how it is." We also assume our memories of events are correct—sort of like a video-recorder putting things into our memory. This is not a good assumption to make. How we see, experience and remember the world has as much to do with how our brain interprets the information coming at it as it does with what's actually happening. Non-ADHD partners need to understand that their brains often filter out important information. So, *for either one of you,* even though you might swear up, down and sideways that something happened a certain way, that still may not have been what actually happened. When it comes to memories, be humble and assume neither of you has the exact story. (For more on this "illusion of attention," see *The Invisible Gorilla* by Chabris and Simons!)

Accepting Your Differences

> **ADHD partner:** *I don't like that (my) ADHD is viewed as a disability… and I am often frustrated by how incredibly linear my wife's thinking is. I get frustrated that she can't seem to make intuitive leaps and that she gets angry with me when I do. For instance, she can't walk into a movie late and quickly pick up the threads of the plot. Instead she needs to ask questions about what happened while she was gone…*

Both individuals from the couple above have their own logic flow. They are a perfect example of "being differently in the world" and are not going to change. He will not become ploddingly logical (as he would think of it), nor will she suddenly learn to make the intuitive leaps that he so easily makes.

Remind yourselves that neither way is "right" or "better." We know that this is a tough idea for some partners to internalize. If you are struggling with it, consider taking some time to meditate on it, journaling your thoughts to work through them, or talking with a friend or family member.

"Trying Harder"

In short, ADHD partners often have a long history of people telling them they should be trying harder. This is truly frustrating because people with ADHD work really, really hard to organize their minds and their lives…even if they don't tell you about it.

Not only do they try hard, they sometimes try hard to accomplish something and fail because an ADHD symptom interfered. As most adults go undiagnosed for much of their lives, this can be confusing. They might wonder, "Why could all of my friends turn in their homework on time while I seemed to always forget it?" or "Why can't I seem to pay more attention to my partner?"

Over time, and with repeated failures, people with undiagnosed ADHD often come to question themselves. The resulting low self-esteem can easily impact decision-making and communication. The thought that *I'll probably fail anyway, so why should I try?* becomes a coping strategy that is hard for a non-ADHD partner to understand.

The unexpected and repeated difficulties that many with ADHD experience growing up are quite different from what those without ADHD often experience. The non-ADHDer's childhood is often one of practicing skills, becoming more accomplished, and eventually gaining confidence that *if I work hard enough, I will probably be able to attain reasonably set goals.*

Be aware of this important difference. Make it safe to try and not immediately succeed in your relationship. And remember that ADHD partners are often trying really hard, even if you can't see it.

Gender Issues

> ***ADHD partner:*** *How much of what is classified as ADHD could also be tagged as "typical dysfunctional male behavior" such as forgetting to call, staying out late after work, etc.?*

Though it's not politically correct to say this, we will. Men and women often approach things differently and this impacts your relationship. Two gender-specific communication issues seem to come up over and over again in our couples counseling:

- Many women find the act of talking things out therapeutic. They like to talk about their feelings and what these feelings mean to them. This is in direct conflict with men, who often seek to fix things and move on. Extended talking can seem beside the point.

- On average it is physiologically harder for a man to be in conflict with a loved one. Research shows that both men and women respond to conflict physiologically with elevated stress chemicals, higher heart rates and faster breathing. Women, however, have the advantage of being faster self-soothers after conflict than men (Parker-Pope, 2010, p. 155-56).

The ramifications of these differences are very specific. Men who listen to their women "talk it out" instead of trying to "fix" the problem have a better chance of ending the conversation on a good note. Sitting tight is a virtue! And women, if you want to discuss a potentially conflict-laden topic with a male partner, creating a low/no conflict environment will increase the chances that your partner will willingly participate.

How to Vent (If You Must!)

1. Ask your partner if this is a good time to vent.
2. If your partner says "no" then come back later.
3. If your partner says "okay," give him a moment to prepare. Then make sure NOT to attack your partner, even if you are struggling to express negative feelings.
4. As much as possible, use "I" language and take responsibility for your feelings, rather than attacking.
5. Ask for problem-solving help at the end of the venting to include your partner in figuring out how to address your concern.

Social Norms

And finally, circling back to the original question about whether behavior stems from ADHD or is just "typical dysfunctional male behavior," we're not convinced that rude or thoughtless behavior is gender related, even though it may be culturally sanctioned by the guys at the office. But perhaps that's just a feminine take on the topic!

Communication Hot Spots–What Couples Say

"Communication" tends to be viewed as synonymous with "getting along." There is a mistaken perception that *if we can just communicate better,* everything will be resolved. That's not accurate. You could communicate perfectly and still not resolve any of your differences.

There is also a sense that *if I could just explain things well enough, my partner would come to see I'm right.* Again, this isn't true. You could be crystal clear and your partner might still think you're wrong! That doesn't negate the need for clear, loving communication. This section tells you how you might get there and highlights specific strategies that work for couples impacted by ADHD.

HOT SPOT 3
Feeling Unloved—Actions vs. Words

Non-ADHD partner: *My husband says he loves me, but his actions say otherwise. He often forgets what we talk about and pays me little attention. How do I get beyond feeling abandoned?*

Non-ADHD partner: *Do you have any suggestions for helping my ADHD partner pay more attention to me? I struggle to connect with him even when he is around, as he seems to be lost in his own world. I feel very much uncared for by him, but he struggles to understand these feelings.*

Distractibility. Chronic tardiness. Difficulty following through on things. Not remembering what the two of you talked about a few weeks ago. Not staying "tuned in" during a conversation. These classic ADHD symptoms all communicate something very negative to a non-ADHD or "other-ADHD" spouse—these actions seem to say *I don't love you.*

You, the ADHD partner, might love your partner more than the moon and the stars put together. You might feel all mushy inside when she walks in. You might feel as if your world would completely fall apart if your partner left you. But trust us when we tell you that what your undermanaged symptomatic behaviors *communicate* is that you don't care.

When your non-ADHD partner comes to you and says she feels lonely or that he feels you don't love him enough or that your lack of involvement in the day-to-day parts of the relationship *hurts,* BELIEVE it! Your partner isn't questioning your love to put on a show. No matter how "in love" you feel, this is NOT the experience your partner is having as long as your symptoms get in the way of your paying attention.

Lack of attention hurts. A lot. In fact, we think it is the number one villain in ADHD-impacted relationships.

Or, if you have conflicted feelings about your partner, but really want to start feeling more positive, understand that paying more attention is a critical component of repairing your relationship.

Saying *I Love You* with "Attend Time"

> **Non-ADHD partner:** *As a non-ADHD spouse, it is hard to not receive the attention I would love to have at the end of an evening. We are working at spending more time together, and my spouse is working on attentiveness, but when the meds wear off, her distraction sets in. Sometimes I don't even get a "good night" or "sleep well" at the end of the day...I want to feel cherished and loved, but right now, I feel like an obligation. Do you have any suggestions?*

It's worth repeating: the ADHD spouse in your partnership may feel love, but distracted behavior doesn't communicate this.

Even though distractibility is one of the leading symptoms of adult ADHD, ADHD partners really *can* pay regular, loving attention to a spouse. Getting good treatment obviously plays a role. (PLEASE read the chapter on good treatment and do the treatment worksheet!) But it's probably not realistic to expect your partner to be able to give you attention at the end of the day when she is both tired and unmedicated. This man would do well to let go of his expectations about this particular time of night (at least temporarily) and find other times when his wife can more readily attend.

Though not the issue for the couple above, sometimes ADHD partners avoid interacting with their partner because they fear that "attending" will not be fun, often with good reason. When a relationship is struggling, many of the interactions with non-ADHD partners are painful, angry or shame-inducing. Why would you want to spend a lot of time talking to your partner when doing so brings on a slew of lectures about how miserable you are or how bad a spouse you have become?

What is *"Attending?"*

"Attending" to your partner means engaging only with your partner in a positive way—one which leaves no doubt in your partner's mind that you care. This might mean making coffee each morning and bringing it up to the bedroom with a smile, making love just the way your partner wants it, or anything positive in between. Going out to dinner with friends, while fun, is not attending since it's not exclusive to the two of you—nor is telling your partner how much she still has to do to be a better partner. While this may be one-on-one time together, it does not unequivocally say I love you.

Sometimes ADHD partners are simply so used to their ADHD symptoms that they can't see beyond them to the heart of what makes a relationship work.

> **ADHD partner:** *I feel ADHD has helped me a great deal, particularly at work. As an ADHD partner, I am usually obsessed with one thing or another that draws my attention away from my partner. How does one communicate caring while so much attention is devoted elsewhere?*

There is an internal conflict in this man's relationship that is actually fairly common. He *likes*, or is at least used to, the idea that his attention is drawn elsewhere. He does not see that it cannot always be elsewhere if he is going to communicate he cares. He would benefit by scheduling time to attend to his wife, and checking in with her once in a while to see if she is happy with the balance he has created.

So non-ADHD or other-ADHD partners often don't get enough attention. Their resulting anger, frustration and pursuit mean that ADHD partners get a lot of attention. Unfortunately, it's the wrong kind!

> **ADHD partner:** *We struggle with a cyclical pattern of my retreating from my husband's pursuit until he blows up…then I'm more attentive again until I can't take the pursuit anymore and the pattern repeats.*

> **Non-ADHD partner:** *I feel really frustrated. I will say something a few times with little or no response from my ADHD partner. Then I will say it more loudly. Finally, I'll just get in his face and yell at him. That gets his attention! But it also makes him mad because he didn't really hear the first attempts. He thinks I'm just yelling at him out of the blue!*

Both of these couples are in pursuit/retreat patterns that originate with inconsistent attention on the part of the ADHD partner. But pursuit is negative attention. ADHD partners often feel they "can't take" the pursuit for long periods of time and either blow up or retreat. And non-ADHD partners find being the pursuer unfulfilling and frustrating. Not only that, pursuit simply doesn't work.

As you can see, "attention" in these cases is not the same thing as "attending." It is the latter you seek. When you clearly communicate your love to your partner by attending to him or her *on a consistent basis and in a loving way that he or she can "hear,"* the result will most likely be that your partner blossoms and becomes happier. And then your partner will turn around and share that happiness back with you. It may not happen overnight, particularly if there are negative emotions and undermanaged ADHD symptoms to deal with, but it will happen. To get there, you must each start to make time to attend to each other. The rest will follow.

Attending Does NOT Mean Everything is Fine

When we suggest to struggling couples that they create more attend time in their relationship, the typical response is mixed. On the intellectual side, they usually see how carving time out to pay more positive attention to each other would help. On the emotional side, they are often more conflicted. Non-ADHD partners, for example, long for attention from their ADHD partner but simultaneously fear that if they act lovingly and "let up on the pressure," then the ADHD partner will "stop trying and revert to poor behaviors." This is not an unfounded fear. In the past, before the ADHD partner was trying to manage the ADHD symptoms *in ways shown to work*, it was difficult for her to sustain attention for more than a couple of weeks. Even the best intentions to finally "try harder to pay attention" were overcome by the ADHD symptoms of distraction, poor memory and more.

On the ADHD partner's side, attention from non-ADHD partners has frequently been negative in nature. "More attention" may have an ominous ring to it, and the ADHD partner may similarly fear that the positive attention will last for a while but then turn into criticism or disappointment. Again, this is not unfounded. Sometimes even the most dedicated non-ADHD partner may become discouraged and engage in "the constant critique" when ADHD symptomatic behaviors continue unabated.

Attend anyway. Jump into paying more positive attention even if you feel these worries. Though you will not be 100% perfect in your efforts, attending will improve your daily interactions. Further, your commitment to being supportive and respectful is the start to rebuilding trust. Positive reinforcement can live side by side with any continuing problems between the two of you. Communicating that you care by creating enough attend time is critically important to addressing those problems. So rather than fear that attending will lead to failure because you still have problems, know that attending is the only way to find success in solving them.

It's Not Just the ADHD Partner's Distraction

We've talked about distractibility and how clearly (and usually unintentionally) ADHD distracted behaviors communicate *I don't love you*. It makes sense to take a few moments and reinforce that it is not just distracted behaviors that get in the way of attend time. By the time couples seek help from us, non-ADHD partners are usually doing some very loud communicating that they don't care, as well. These are just a few of the ways they regularly communicate *I don't love you* to their ADHD partners:

- Criticism
- Disapproval and disappointment
- Nagging and suggesting that the ADHD partner isn't competent
- Chronic anger and frustration

- Verbal abuse
- Contempt
- Disengagement
- Punishment
- Negative pursuit
- Constant attempts to "educate" and correct

These are exceptionally common non-ADHD (or other-ADHD) responses in the symptom/response/response patterns of the *ADHD Effect*. However, they are incredibly destructive to a relationship and your ability to communicate well together. We can't address all of these responses here (see the other book for more information) but want to remind you of them because we don't want either of you getting the impression that we are only picking on the ADHD partner!

How To Attend Well Enough

Have we convinced you yet that having enough time for "attending" is critical—and that one must attend in a loving way? Do you realize that there is *no* way you will thrive if you don't get this right? We hope so! Here are some specific strategies you can use to add more of the right kind of "attend time" to your relationship:

- **Schedule regular blocks of time to be together.** You can figure out what you are doing during that time later. For example, set aside 1-4 p.m. every Saturday afternoon to explore your city. At 1:00, no matter what, stop what you are doing and decide what sounds like fun for those few hours. Look on the computer for that day's local happenings and festivals. Find a concert or museum to go to. Walk hand in hand around the park. Explore the farmer's market together. Spend an afternoon skiing together. If you have kids, get a sitter or set up a reciprocal child exchange with friends. If afternoons don't work, make it a regular evening date night that you do *no matter what.*

- **Create regular "little routines"** that say *I love you and want to be with you* to your partner. In the Orlov household, one of those routines is George making coffee for Melissa in the morning, and Melissa making breakfast. For Melissa's parents, it was doing the *NY Times* crossword puzzle together each night before bed. In Nancie's household, Nancie and Steve take a late night stroll with their dogs, often catching up on the day's events or planning for the next day. There are a lot of little routines you can set up in your day to help you show that you care.
- **Say "I love you" at least once every day.** If you need to set a reminder, do so!
- **Set up "attend time" at bedtime.** If you and your partner have wildly different bedtimes and sleeping patterns, create a nighttime routine that gets you into the bedroom at the same time. Take some time to talk, hold each other, read together or just be together. When the earlier-to-bed partner is ready to turn out the lights, the later-to-bed partner can decide whether he/she wants to stay, or get up and do something else.
- **Consider "cuddle time."** Couples who are having trouble feeling intimately connected can benefit from creating 10-15 minutes of non-sexual cuddle time at night or in the morning. Set your alarm 10 minutes early (or go to bed earlier) so that you can hold each other. This is time to feel the connection of touch, say nice things to each other, or just experience the joy of being near your partner without any pressure. It's a very positive way to start or finish your day.

- **Create a 5-minute no complaints rule.** When you walk in the door after a hard day, spend five minutes in the same room talking about positive things that happened that day. This makes the transition back home easier while also reinforcing a positive tone to your relationship.
- **Say "thank you" whenever you can.** Positive words are an important form of "attend time." Say thank you whenever you can. It takes about two seconds to say, and appreciation is critical to joyous relationships.
- **Don't respond to individual annoyances, just to larger patterns**. Sometimes your partner will do something that bugs you. Let it go unless you see a pattern developing over a period of a couple of weeks. So, for example, if Melissa is cranky one day, George won't mention it. If she throws her weight around for a week, though, he will ask her what is going on and gently remind her that he likes the loving and friendly version of her better. Think of yourself as Teflon—unless there is something meaningful that sticks like Velcro over time.
- **Surprise your partner by planning something she has told you she would love to do.** Make sure it's something you've heard your partner say she wants. If you have ADHD, make a habit of jotting down a note on your cell phone when she says, "I wish we could…" Nancie remembers how excited she was when Steve surprised her with tickets to the Orange County Science Center after she had once mentioned it in passing. Not only did he remember, he even wrapped the tickets up as a Christmas present!
- **Set a reminder to plan.** Schedule a repeating weekly "event" on your cell phone calendar to remind you to take 15 minutes to research and plan something new and interesting to do together, perhaps during the time you've set aside to be together (see the first bullet!).

- **Create reset weekends.** This is harder when there are kids around, though friends or grandparents can babysit. The idea is to get away from it all by immersing yourselves in each other for 48 hours. One friend of Melissa's goes sailing with her husband for two or three days at a time. Another idea would be to get a hotel room in the city and create a sort of extended date. Or you can go hiking and camping for a weekend. There are lots of options. *Resetting* every once in a while can really help.

Other Secrets of Attend Time

Attend time is so important that we have to keep going! Here are some secrets about why attend time is so critical to your ability to thrive together:

Attending to your partner in a loving way is in your own best interests. When people feel loved, they are more likely to be generous with their feelings in return. However, if the ADHD partner in your couple remains too distracted to properly reciprocate attention, take the high road. Talk lovingly about not feeling well enough attended, and collaboratively brainstorm ways to share more attend time.

Attend time is about engaging. It's not about physically being in the same room. Sitting at the counter and working on the computer while your partner cooks does not adequately communicate you care, even if the reason you moved there was to help her feel less lonely.

Do new and challenging things together. One quick way to build connections is to do new and challenging things together. Just spending time together doesn't improve your connection nearly as well.

Reliability is a critical factor in clearly communicating your love. Your gestures don't need to be grand gestures of love if they are communicated *regularly and clearly*. You don't have to attend perfectly, but the "norm" needs to be a regular, understandable communication of the idea *I love you*.

Other Ways to Say I Love You–Validation and Reliability

We've written a lot about attend time because it's a really important part of thriving together. You want to make sure, even when one or both partners is often distracted, that you get enough time together in a way that communicates *I love you and choose to be with you.* But there are two other ways to communicate that idea which we would like to bring to your attention.

The Art of Validation

Validating your partner's opinions is a great way to show your respect and care. Couples often assume that "validation" is the same thing as "agreement." This is not the case. Validation simply means you acknowledge that your partner has the right to his or her own opinion and logic flow. Even if you completely disagree with your partner, you can still validate her.

Let us give you some examples. Say one partner isn't following through on household tasks, leaving his partner with all of the work. She says resentfully, "I feel like the household slave!" Here are some familiar responses to that comment:

- *You're not!*
- *You're better at this stuff than I am!*
- *The stuff you are doing isn't necessary; therefore I'm not obligated to help out.*
- *(No comment. Goes to other room.)*

The first two comments might sound like good, supportive responses—but they aren't. They are *invalidating* because they completely ignore what the speaker has just said! When you validate someone, you listen to what her opinion is and acknowledge it. You may not understand why your partner feels like the household slave, or you may not agree that she ought to, but to tell her she isn't—right after she has just told you she is—

completely invalidates her feelings. She will come away from that exchange feeling resentful that you never listen to her and believing that you simply *don't get it!*

Leaving the room or not responding is equally problematic. Your partner has just expressed something that is important to her. Avoiding conflict by leaving communicates *I don't care what you think.* Though we understand how difficult responding to these kinds of comments can be, engagement with your partner's feelings is better than disengagement over the long run. You don't have to solve the problem right now, but *acknowledging* she has expressed it, and that she has a right to express it, is an important element of partnership.

So let's try this exchange again, this time offering possible responses that are validating instead of invalidating. When she says, "I feel like the household slave!" you might respond:

- *I didn't know that.* (neutral but acknowledging her point of view)
- *You do? Why?* (neutral…interested in the idea)
- *I know I'm not doing as much as you would like me to. I'm sorry.* (acknowledgement and apology)
- *I wouldn't want to feel that way either. Are there ways to help out?* (empathy and offer to change the status quo)
- *That must make you feel resentful. Can we talk about what chores you are doing? I'm wondering if you might be taking on more than you need to.* (acknowledgement and disagreement)
- *You've been saying that for a while now. I guess we should talk about what to do about it.* (acknowledgement with promise to pursue…but not necessarily resolve)
- *I understand you feel like you do all the work around here, but I would like to respectfully disagree with that…* (acknowledgement and disagreement)

Even though these statements are all different—some are neutral, some are agreeing, some disagreeing—they have some aspects in common. They are all respectful, and they all start from the statement of the original speaker by acknowledging her point of view. That's validation.

Sometimes it's hard to figure out how to validate your partner.

> ***ADHD partner:*** *Can you illustrate a constructive, validating response an ADHD partner can give when the other partner is implicitly critical and controlling?*

Critical and controlling behavior is common among non-ADHD partners who feel their lives are out of control due to ADHD issues. They feel they are not being heard, that the ADHD partner is not managing his/her symptoms as well as the non-ADHD partner would like. So they may criticize and control because they want things to improve. Here are some possible responses that validate in spite of the criticism. Use them simply as a starting point for thinking about your own specific situation:

> ***Non-ADHD husband:*** *Once again you've missed the deadline we agreed to, so now I'm going to have to pick up the pieces and do it myself!*

> ***ADHD wife:*** *I hear how hard it is for you when I don't do something that I said I would do. It's frustrating for me, too. In fact, I'm putting the following plan in place to address this specific issue. I realize this problem is occurring in other situations, too. So please understand that I hear you and am trying to respond in a meaningful, long-term way. I simply ask that you stop being so critical of me while I work on the problem. I'm happy to hear your concerns, but it's hard for me when you are so negative. I'm asking you to give me time to work this out.*

In this example, the ADHD partner agrees that her behavior is a problem. Her response is validating because it shows she heard the frustration, has internalized the problem enough to extrapolate to other similar situations and, furthermore, is planning to respond. She also asks—in a polite way—for the non-ADHD partner to back off.

She might *not* agree, though. In that case, one validating response might be this one:

> ***ADHD wife:*** *I understand that you don't like the fact that I missed the deadline. It seems that the reason you don't like it is that it puts a lot of extra work on your shoulders. So I hear what you are saying, but I don't happen to agree with you—I don't think you need to take on this project right now. I did miss the deadline, but I have set aside two hours this Tuesday evening to finish the work. I just couldn't get to it yet.*

This response indicates a clear understanding of the distress expressed in the criticism but also pushes back on the assumption that this means more work for the non-ADHD partner. While the non-ADHD partner might not like that he has to wait for another couple of days, the ADHD partner remains responsible for the work and has a specific plan for completion. It is the right of the ADHD partner to choose when and how to complete the project. Now it's her job to actually do it. If she delays and delays, then a different issue arises—one about whether or not she has her symptoms managed well enough to be reliable. A short delay doesn't impact this...but numerous delays would. (If her choice is to complete the project a year from now, then a different conversation is in order so the non-ADHD partner isn't left in the lurch!)

Think about your own interactions with your partner. How many times have you unwittingly invalidated your partner's opinion? We're guessing quite a few. You may have even used a warm, loving tone of voice when doing so! Saying, "Honey, you shouldn't feel that way," misses the main point—*she does*. Emotions are not just a matter of will. They need empathy and love, not correction.

To help partners understand how much they validate and invalidate each other, we offer a two-day validation exercise in the back of this book. This exercise was originally released in *The ADHD Effect on Marriage* but deserves reprinting here. Try it—we think it will be an eye opener for you!

"Reliable Enough" Says I Love You

We alluded to the idea that reliability is a critical factor in building a strong relationship—and that ADHD symptoms definitely interfere with reliability! It's safe to say that *from a relationship perspective,* the whole *point* of treating ADHD is to make sure that the ADHD partner is *reliable enough* in the relationship.

That does *NOT* mean that the goal is for the ADHD partner to become or act like the partner who does not have ADHD. This is simply not going to happen! You are two unique individuals with two different brains and two different approaches. An ADHD partner will contribute to the partnership in his or her own particular way.

That said, *reliable enough* is a critical concept. No partner, ADHD or not, needs to be perfect. On the other hand, a healthy relationship includes the idea that each partner can rely on the other without constantly feeling up in the air, wondering *will my partner remember? Will my partner follow through? Will I continue to feel loved, or is this just a spurt of hyperfocus?* The norm in the relationship needs to be that both partners are reliable enough to be trustworthy, a concept we write more about on page 193. For ADHD partners, trying to manage symptoms (of distractibility, feeling overwhelmed, poor memory and more) and getting the structures in place to create that reliability can be a real challenge. But the process of doing so communicates something really important: *This may be hard, but I love you and want to be a good partner to you. This effort is my love letter to us both.*

To all the ADHD partners out there who are working hard to become (or remain) reliable enough, we salute your efforts. To all the non-ADHD partners who are watching these efforts (perhaps with trepidation!), we hope you are acknowledging how much work this takes and are reiterating that you "hear" that this effort is an expression of love.

HOT SPOT 4
Too Many Hurtful Fights

All couples fight. It's part of being together. What differentiates healthy couples from unhealthy couples are two things: *how* they fight, and how they *repair* from a fight.

> **ADHD partner:** *I am doing my best to stay calm when my wife, who doesn't have ADHD, nags me over and over about the same things all the time. But somehow it just seems that I can't help but get mad. She just gets to me. We seem to fight all the time. Once we get started, she gets really angry too, and it just seems to keep on going. I love her, but these fights are really taking their toll on me. I just can't take much more of this. It's so exhausting, I need to take a nap when it's all over, and then she gets mad at that.*

> **ADHD partner:** *My husband just doesn't get it. It's true that I'm a stay-at-home mom, and he goes out to work every day. But when he comes home, all I hear is how everything is a mess and he can't understand what I've been doing all day. The next thing you know, we're fighting about whose job is harder, and his attitude crushes me. I have ADHD, and it seems like no matter how hard I try, with three kids, I just can't get enough done in a day to make him happy. It doesn't seem to matter that the kids are fed and doing okay. No, that's not good enough for him. If there's a dish in the sink, or the bed isn't made, I've somehow failed my "job." The fighting is awful. Can't he see I'm doing my best?*

Non-ADHD partner: *Couples who aren't dealing with ADHD fight and get through it. Why can't we?*

Non-ADHD partner: *Though I know that fighting can be unproductive, as a non-ADHD spouse, it is very hard for me to just walk away during an argument. I feel ignored, like he is not listening, and when he gets angry it can be explosive and out of control. This gets me even more frustrated. Sometimes when I try to walk away, he is in such a rage that he tries to keep going. When I do walk away, he expects me to just forget about it and not discuss the issue. Things may get better, but then they end up blowing up again. What is the best approach when I feel that no matter how I approach my ADHD partner he gets defensive and angry?*

What are the best approaches? Why do other couples get through this when you don't? These are great questions. Happily, research into relationships can help provide the answers.

What the Science Says About Fighting

John Gottman, Ph.D., and his associates have done a great deal of research on healthy relationships. Their work suggests that it's not how often you fight that indicates the health of a marriage. Rather, it's the actions you take when you fight and how you repair from a fight that predict marital stability. So we will review what makes a "good" fight—i.e., one that doesn't damage your relationship. We will also cover ways to repair from fights and, happily, how to avoid some of the worst.

Turning Your Arguments into "Good Fights"

Fighting is an indicator that something needs to be attended to. But there are ways to have "good" fights, fights that focus on airing your disagreements rather than blowing up at each other. Many of these concepts for fighting well are based on the research of Gottman and his associates, and we send you to Gottman and Silver's *The Seven Principles for Making a Marriage Work* if you are interested in more in-depth information about their findings and resulting marriage therapy suggestions. The book is filled with worksheets, lots more background on their research, and many usable tactics.

We believe that if you try incorporating these ideas into your conflicts, you will start to see improvements in your interactions. Be open with your partner about the fact that you are trying them and encourage him or her to do the same:

- **Start your conversation with a complaint, not a criticism.** "I'm concerned that the garbage isn't getting taken out regularly," is a complaint. "You never take out the garbage as you promised you would," is a criticism. Complaints work better because they are more respectful and because they don't put the listener on the defensive as quickly. It is important to notice the use of "I" language at the beginning of the complaint versus the "you" language of the criticism.
- **Soft starts are the way to go.** A soft start is when you ease into a topic without attack. Soft starts show respect by not making assumptions and tend to include observations rather than criticisms. They also focus more on the feelings of the speaker than on the actions of the person being spoken to. Here are some examples. Notice that the statements say the same thing, but come across quite differently:

  Hard start: *You never pay attention to me.*

  Soft start: *I really miss you! We aren't spending enough time together these days.*

  Hard start: *You have to help me this weekend with the garden —the fence is broken again. Remember you said you would? The deer are stomping all over it.*

Soft start: *I'm sad to see that the flowers are getting eaten again! Would you help me in the garden this weekend? It's been so long since we worked on it.*

- **Be respectful.** No matter how hard the topic, or how upset you are, your partner ALWAYS deserves respect. Always!
- **Use non-threatening words and don't bully your partner.** In a good relationship, partners have similar levels of power to influence each other and make decisions. Threatening words and postures, even during arguments, detract from that idea. Bullying your partner is an attempt to put your partner down and make him/her less powerful. Such behavior is always negative and quickly builds resentment in your partner.
- **Use clarifying phrases.** We've already talked about how different you are. It helps to clarify what you mean, particularly if your partner looks confused or doesn't seem to be responding as you expect. "So what I mean is that I'm really frustrated by our mutual inability to get the kids to school on time," is an example of a succinct clarifying phrase.
- **Talk calmly.** This is another version of being respectful. When you are calm, your partner may be better able to hear you and respond. Further, you are able to think through your thoughts more carefully if you aren't angry. Breathing deeply can help you stay calm.
- **Use verbal cues to de-escalate your interactions.** We review how to set these up later in this chapter.
- **Look for common ground.** You are more likely to stay constructively engaged if you focus on similarities and shared concerns.
- **Look your partner in the eye**. This serves a dual purpose —it communicates quite a bit about how you feel and also ensures that you have each other's full attention.

- **Ask open-ended questions.** The best fights are actually conversations in which you happen to disagree. Rather than lecturing your partner, remember to invite him or her into the conversation by asking questions that request a reaction such as, "Do you see it that way?" or "What do you think?" Then, really listen to your partner's response.
- **Use affirming statements.** Even if you disagree with your partner on something, you can still validate him or her.
- **Accept the legitimacy of negative emotions.** Rather than fighting against the negative emotions, commiserate with your partner.
- **Soothe your partner when you can.** Women, specifically, can strategically soothe their partner during a fight in order to de-escalate the interaction. Soothing techniques include agreement, approval, humor, touch, seeking common ground, apologizing and validating.

The ideas in this list may seem obvious, but it's surprising how easy it is to move away from using them when you are in conflict. It takes thought to use affirming statements and ask open-ended questions when you are feeling frustrated and want to prove your point! But it really is important. It's not the words, specifically, but the emotional nature of what's behind them. If you are unable to treat your partner with respect, your relationship will never thrive. Eventually, it may well end.

Coming Back Later

When you must postpone an important conversation, make sure that you get back to it by: 1.) assuring your partner you will get back to the topic and 2.) immediately creating a reminder to do so in your reminder system. A large note left in an obvious place (next to the sink in the bathroom or on the kitchen counter) works, too.

Can We Repair Past Damage? The ADHD Relationship Specifics

You may think that you will never be able to repair the damage that has been done to your relationship. Let us reassure you—you can! Here's why:

- A lot of the past issues were related to not knowing about the *ADHD Effect* and not having the tools necessary to improve your relationship. But **now you have a wide array of better strategies** or are in the process of acquiring them.
- You can't "redo" your past together, as much as you might like to, but you can **choose to forgive yourself and your partner**. You did the best you could with very incomplete information, and you responded naturally and predictably to the pressures undiagnosed or undermanaged ADHD symptoms placed upon you. Forgiveness for that can free you from your past and enable you to move forward more positively than you might imagine.
- You have learned to **separate the symptoms from the person with ADHD.** It is a *fact* that with effort and treatment ADHD is manageable for most people. As you start to use your new tools and attack the symptoms, not the person, your interactions will get better and better.
- By rigorously **scheduling *attend time***, you now know how to fill the void that is left when you *eliminate* negative interactions: you fill it with positive interactions that remind you of why you love each other.
- **You can practice how to have "good fights"** and make your disagreements much more productive.
- You are **learning the art of validating** each other. This is a critical skill for repairing after conflict.

Making Up and "Soothing"

You will continue to have fights, at least some of the time. So you need to know how to recover. Gottman's work suggests that offering and accepting "bids for repair" is critical to the health of your relationship. But it is very hard to predict exactly which repair behaviors will work for which couples. In other words, while we can provide you with a list of ideas, you may need to experiment to see which strategies work for you. As an example, doing something funny might smooth over the worst offenses for some couples, while for others the use of humor in a serious moment would add to the problem.

Either partner can offer the repair behavior. Here's one hilarious example: one day Melissa backed out of the garage and hit George's car. She was mortified and emotional while he was angry and chewing her out. As an interaction, it wasn't going very well…plus, that long, dented stripe of red paint down the side of George's white car…ugh! Then George remembered a several-day-old bouquet of flowers in his trunk that he had forgotten to give her. This reminded him that they both make mistakes, so he opened the trunk and presented Melissa with the badly wilted (okay, almost dead!) flowers and apologized for getting mad at her. This reminded *her* that they both make mistakes and soon both were laughing instead of arguing.

Dead flowers might not work to calm your partner, but here are some olive branches you might offer:

- **An apology.**
- **Participating in anything that stops a conversation from escalating out of control** (for example, verbal cues). Working to stop the conversation (even if you do so angrily) shows you care.
- **Telling your partner that you are feeling out of control**, taking the time to calm yourself, then returning to the conversation later in a more constructive way.

- **Admitting you are partially or completely wrong**—*You're right, there is no excuse for my speaking to you in that tone of voice, no matter how frustrated I am.*
- **Talking about reconsidering your partner's point of view**—*I hadn't thought of it that way…give me a moment to consider that.*
- **Generalizing the conversation** to move it away from details and find common ground—*So even though we disagree on the details, we are both really saying we hate being so busy.*
- **Using statements that move you towards agreement** or more constructive negotiation, such as *Perhaps we can include both of our ideas while we figure out the solution.*
- **Statements that remind you that you are both on the same team**—*Though we're arguing, I know we both want what's best for our son. Let's see if we can approach this a different way or let's try to approach this as members of the same team…how about if we alternate taking responsibility?*
- **Showing appreciation**—*I don't agree with all of your conclusions, but I really appreciate how much time you're taking to try to convince me of your opinion. That shows how much you care!*
- **Approaching a problem from your partner's organizational perspective**—*I'm not sure we're tracking together. What do you think about creating a list of ideas?*
- **Agreeing to disagree**—Since 70% of issues are unresolvable in the long run, this can be very useful… as long as it's not used as a way to brush off your partner's opinion: *We've been talking about this issue for days and reached no resolution. Can we agree to disagree and see if we can create a work-around?* The action statement here is useful—you aren't saying *drop it*, but rather, *let's approach this differently.*

- **Staying neutral**—Stating your case in a neutral way, rather than a negative one, can be as useful as actually saying positive words.
- **Rephrasing**—Particularly if your partner seems to be shutting down or stuck in tunnel vision, consider completely rephrasing what you are trying to say. Make sure you use soft starts and constructive, respectful language when you do. Better yet, rephrase what you thought you heard your partner say to check your comprehension.
- **Being willing to be swayed by your female partner's opinion**—Gottman's research suggests men who are willing to be influenced by their partners contribute to a strong relationship. Relationships in which men are *unwilling* to be influenced by their female partners may well end up in divorce. (His research suggests that women's willingness to be influenced by men makes little difference in divorce rates.)

When your partner offers up one of these ways of smoothing out your interaction, TAKE IT!

Compromising with Your Partner

When it comes to good fights, it's important to understand that more than half of your fights are *unresolvable*—they result from deep down differences in opinion or approach. A common non-ADHD/ADHD difference, for example, has to do with what constitutes "adequately organized" as relates to planning events, organizing a household, raising children and the like. Another is whether or not you should let things "just happen" (be spontaneous) or whether you should actively "make them happen" (plan ahead and pursue set goals). Those with ADHD typically have a higher tolerance for spontaneity and disorganization, perhaps because they've had so much more experience with it.

If you have been talking about the same issues for many years, it may be time to take a different approach and create a work-around. The reality is there are two of you, and compromise is often necessary. Compromise does not mean "give up" or "lower my standards." It means accepting you are different and figuring out how to move forward with your lives while accommodating those differences.

Here are some examples from Nancie's and Melissa's lives that help illustrate this:

- George likes to hang on to stuff *because it might be useful in the future, who knows,* and doesn't worry too much about how it's organized. Melissa likes things more tidy than that. After years of discussion, their work-around includes hiring someone to help clean the house every other week (so Melissa doesn't bear all of the burden of cleaning up) and to separate out key spaces. She no longer worries about, nor comments upon, what he keeps in his specific areas of their home—his office, closet, or bathroom area, his side of the garage or the basement. Their bedroom can also be messy. George, for his part, helps keep the public spaces of their home tidy.
- Like many with ADHD, Steve is a late night person who often comes to bed after 1 a.m. This used to drive Nancie crazy. For the longest time, Nancie tried to impress upon Steve how important it was that they be in bed at the same time. Many uncomfortable conversations led to Steve feeling controlled and Nancie feeling hurt and baffled by his late night habits. Now, Steve gets into bed a couple of nights a week at the same time as Nancie, and they almost daily spend some time together in the mornings when they awaken. This gives them *together time,* which is what Nancie wanted, while respecting Steve's desires, too. Nancie has learned to enjoy her quiet reading time before lights out on the nights when Steve stays up later, so she has turned a negative into a positive.

- Both George and Melissa find that sometimes they slip into bad habits, such as being overly critical or becoming more emotional than the situation warrants. Rather than engage negatively at these times, they've developed verbal cues that alert both partners to what is happening. These cues remind them to stop all conversation and regroup later.

Work-arounds and effective compromises require conversation and engagement. But they also take setting some boundaries. There are—very rarely—times when compromise is not appropriate. We draw a bright, uncrossable line at all types of physical abuse or behavior that puts members of the household at unnecessary risk (particularly children). We also have very strong opinions that respectful behavior should be the default in your relationship.

Knowing what's non-negotiable can help you solve specific problems you face. For example, couples ask us with surprising frequency what to do when an ADHD partner can't remember to put medications away in a household that includes young children. The ADHD partner says, "I'm trying…" and the non-ADHD partner says, "I know, but you left our child's medication out again…you need to do better!" In this case, waiting to develop a new skillset is not as important as the potential catastrophe of an accidental overdose. The couple needs to immediately create a solution that *eliminates* the danger. That likely means the non-ADHD partner needs to take over giving medication to the kids and accept that this is just "one of those things."

As you think about compromise, we urge you to discuss your values and boundaries. It's important to understand what you are completely unwilling to compromise on. Make sure this list is short and genuinely important to you as an individual. The list should include "bright line" issues, such as not putting your children at physical risk or striking a partner, as well as those things you simply cannot give up, such as being treated with respect. *Everything* else is negotiable.

Avoiding a Fight by Using Verbal Cues

We're guessing you would also like to fight less! Learning to use verbal cues can help.

Some fights you can see coming and are particularly difficult. You've been down this same road many times before, and you can see yourself or your partner getting worked up. You fear that you will get into one of those flooded arguments in which you lose all ability to control yourselves. At that point, your conversation is almost guaranteed to be hurtful and unproductive, as there is no logical way to communicate. (We include information about flooding in Hot Spot 11, page 110.) Verbal cues can help you keep from going there.

Verbal cues are simply a set of words that two partners agree to use to improve the direction of an interaction they are having. Verbal cues, and their close "cousins," physical cues, can be used for more than just stopping fights. You might use them to:

- **Secretly communicate**—The ADHD partner gets very noisy after a few drinks at a party and starts to offend people but doesn't read the body language cues to realize this. A non-ADHD partner observes this and uses an agreed upon physical cue (a quick tap on the arm) to let him know so he can decide whether or not to wrap up what he is saying.
- **Gently "reset" a conversation**—During a conversation, Melissa gets distracted by something outside a nearby window. George notices and says, "Squirrel!" (a reference to the loveable but easily distracted dog in the movie *Up*). Both of them realize she got distracted and George is calling her on it. They laugh at the reference and return to their conversation.
- **Stay in a conversation**—A woman loses track of a conversation in the middle of it and says, "I'm sorry, I just zoned out for a minute. Can you repeat that?"

Her life partner repeats what he just said. This cue allows the woman with ADHD to jump back in the conversation without missing anything.

- **Notify others about external mood issues**—Melissa is feeling grumpy and starts to be short-tempered with her family. Her kids joke with her, "Uh oh, mean mom's back!" She takes a quick look at what she's just been saying, realizes she's in a bad mood, and apologizes. Then she readjusts her attitude so she doesn't ruin everyone's day.
- **Notify others about internal mood issues**—Nancie and Steve are talking about their mutual responsibilities. Suddenly, the conversation starts to feel overwhelming to Nancie. She raises her hand and says, "Hold on, I'm starting to feel overwhelmed. Can we come back to this tonight?" Steve, who didn't realize she was feeling overwhelmed, stops what he is saying and gives Nancie time to recover her composure. They talk after dinner, instead.
- **Stop a conversation from escalating out of control**—A couple is talking about going to an extended family get-together, which is always a touchy subject for them. One of them starts to feel that the conversation is getting negative and is about to spin out of control. She uses a verbal cue to stop it, let them both regroup, and readdress the issue in a more positive way.

As you can see, verbal cues are a flexible and very useful tool. To be effective, though, they must include these parts:

1. **Agreement that there is a repetitive problem** that a cue can address. Verbal cues don't work if they are imposed on one partner by the other—both must participate willingly!
2. **Agreement to a goal**—what do you want to accomplish with the verbal cue?

3. **A conversation about how the cue will work:**
   – What the cue is (specific words or actions)
   – What it means
   – What the response will be

Agreeing to a specific response to a verbal cue is just as important as setting the cue. If Melissa's response to George's use of "Squirrel!" was, "Take a hike, buddy, I'm not the distracted one, you are!" (rather than laughing about her distraction and returning to the conversation) the cue would be ineffective.

So here's an example. Jesse (ADHD) and Dina (non-ADHD) get into huge arguments when she starts to talk about her concerns that Jesse isn't taking good care of their daughter, Allie. Jesse spends a lot of time with Allie and sees himself as a good dad, though admits he's often not on time and doesn't always enforce any specific bedtime, preferring to play with Allie as long as Allie can stay awake. Dina feels strongly that Allie should be raised with (among other things) the discipline of a regular bedtime, so she keeps bringing up her feelings that Jesse should be doing things differently. As he ignores her point of view, she becomes more distressed, and the fight turns into one about her feeling ignored and his feeling she's always trying to control him. They have a growing number of arguments about both the bedtime question and the larger issues of control and attention in which Jesse explodes and Dina ends up in tears. Finally, they agree that neither one of them wants to continue this pattern and decide to set up a verbal cue. This mutual agreement is the first step in creating an effective cue.

They sit down when not arguing and talk about their goals—to stop escalating into these fights and to find a different way to discuss this issue of control. They decide upon the cue "chili pepper." They choose this nonsensical cue because they feel it will stand out more than saying something like "I'm feeling overwhelmed" or "this isn't going so well." Furthermore, their first date was at a Mexican restaurant, so these words remind them of being happy together.

As a next step, they discuss what "chili pepper" means and decide it stands for, "We are about to get into another really destructive fight. We love each other and don't want to do that, so we will stop talking about this issue and come back to it this evening right after dinner. In the meantime, we will both think about ways to express our concerns so they don't feel like an attack."

Notice that they have agreed to specific next steps as part of their cue. If they didn't have that, then the cue would stop the conversation, but they would never get a chance to discuss their mutual issues, and either one might grow more and more resentful. So make sure, when setting a cue, that you agree to what the response action and follow-up will be.

Jesse and Dina can use this verbal cue any time their fights start to escalate out of control. If they continue to differ, even when they are able to negotiate in calmer ways, then it may be time to talk with a marriage counselor.

We urge you all to consider how verbal or physical cues might help you smooth out your relationship. They are a critical part of helping couples learn to thrive!

HOT SPOT 5
Listening, Comprehension, and Short-Term Memory Issues

We've talked about how different you are, and how that could be one reason why you hear and experience things so differently. But there might be other reasons, too. First, distractibility may impair an ADHD partner's ability to listen carefully. There are so many other interesting (or at least obtrusive!) things going on at the same time! Second, if you are not hearing all the words your partner is saying, it's likely you also won't catch all the nuances and get the full meaning of those words. Third, even if the conversation is completely understood, many with ADHD have difficulty with short-term memory. When they go to retrieve the information from the conversation for later use, it is either incomplete or not there at all. These issues can create conflict, hurt, confusion and embarrassment.

> ***ADHD partner:*** *I have inattentive ADHD. Often, even though I appear to understand what my husband is saying, I actually don't. I might seem very involved in a conversation and not even realize I'm missing anything, but later, when something related comes up, I don't make the connection. How do I deal with this when I don't realize I'm missing things in the first place?*

> ***ADHD partner:*** *Sometimes we have these ongoing conversations that drag on for a long time. Each time we come back to the conversation, I feel lost and can't get back into it. My partner gets very frustrated. Any suggestions?*

> **Non-ADHD partner:** *My partner often forgets conversations we have had—sometimes very recent conversations. Three weeks ago we had this amazing conversation about some issues really important to me. At the time I thought things were getting better, but now he doesn't remember. He doesn't even remember we had the conversation! That really hurts because this was important stuff to me and now we're back to square one. How can he remember better?*

Happily, even if these symptoms persist, there are specific tactics that couples can use to alleviate the issues that they cause. Before reviewing the tactics, though, let us reiterate that *poor comprehension or memory is not personal.* The fact that your partner doesn't remember your important emotional conversation does not mean that it wasn't also important to him or her, or that your partner doesn't love you. You may be able to make peace with this idea if you return to the concept of separating the symptoms from the person.

To respond, the two of you can create a system that will a.) increase the likelihood that important information is not lost and b.) create a safe environment for handling confusion or hurt. This means creating external memory aids as well as increasing patience with memory or distraction issues.

The idea is to capture data and memories outside your head, since your internal memory is relatively weak. One possible strategy for this is writing things down. Melissa sometimes suggests to her ADHD clients that important conversations end with writing key points into a journal. The journal can then be left out and referred to intermittently as a way to remind the ADHD partner of what's going on in the relationship. If an important topic comes up that the partner doesn't remember, she can go back to the journal quickly to refresh her memory.

In non-ADHD relationships, this solution might seem clunky. But in this case, it's just a work-around for an identifiable symptom. Wishing that the ADHD partner would remember better doesn't get you very far. Something else has to be done.

Another option (and perhaps the easier to implement) is for the ADHD partner to "borrow" the memory of a non-ADHD partner. By using the verbal cue "I don't remember that conversation, can you quickly recap it for me?" or something similar, a person with ADHD can quickly be brought back up to speed on important points. This option, of course, takes full and empathetic (or at least neutral) participation on the part of the non-ADHD partner. If he or she resents having to reiterate the details, then this system will be neither reliable nor long-lasting. It also takes trust on the part of the ADHD partner, for it is based upon the assumption that the non-ADHD partner will recap the past conversation as accurately as he or she is able.

This is a great example of how couples can change an interaction that has typically been very negative in the past into something that is positive and supportive. It recognizes the ADHD symptom and compassionately solves the problems that both partners experience as a result of that symptom's expression. The ADHD partner is able to reenter the conversation gracefully, and both are able to pick up where they left off. Is it as ideal as both partners being able to remember exactly what happened? Obviously not. But it's realistic and works well *as long as it's fully embraced by both partners.*

More Memory and Comprehension Boosters

There are a slew of ideas you can use to improve memory, listening and comprehension in a conversation. And trust us when we tell you we are *not* just talking about what the ADHD partner hears and interprets! It's highly likely you *both* can use help hearing what your partner is trying to tell you. Here are tactics that increase the likelihood of physically hearing each other:

Memory Training Programs

There are a number of computer programs designed by neurologists to help people strengthen their short-term memory. Some of the most famous, including CogMed, Lumosity, and Cognifit, make strong claims about the efficacy of their product, which they back up with research. In the spirit of "try whatever you can afford that won't hurt you," you may wish to use one of these programs. However, a meta-analysis which was reported in Barkley's *ADHD Report* in 2013, suggests it may not help. Once all of the research with poor research methodology or very small sample sizes is eliminated, the data suggests that "working memory training has positive effects on tasks similar to those trained...but there is no evidence of a transfer to other less directly related tasks." Further, they suggest that there is little evidence that these programs are "suitable treatments for developmental disorders (such as ADHD or dyslexia)." (Melby-Lervag & Hulme, 2013, p. 1-5)

That said, that research did not separate out the coached products from the self-study programs. Experience at the Hallowell Center in Sudbury, MA would suggest that the coached programs (they offer CogMed) can provide solid progress that lasts. And being able to pull things such as numbers and patterns out of your memory, which is what these programs work on, may be beneficial. In addition, making measurable progress from start to finish in a program can boost confidence—helping instill a more "can do" attitude in the person doing the training. This may be a benefit that the research simply doesn't examine.

Listening and Comprehension Ideas

- **Review and use the "good fights" list of ways to engage in conflict.** One reason people have difficulty hearing what you are saying is that they feel on the defensive and are, therefore, tuned out.
- **Be in the same room**. It does not work to communicate by yelling across the house! Words get garbled or not heard at all.
- **Look each other in the eye.** You have the greatest likelihood of having your ADHD partner's full attention when he is looking you in the eye.
- **Wait to speak until your partner is ready.** If your partner is writing an important email, it's unlikely she is going to get the full gist of what you are trying to say.
- **Make it okay not to interact.** Melissa uses the verbal cue, "Is this an okay time to talk?" when interrupting George during a workday. If he's too busy he says, "Not right now," and they come back to it later. If she insisted they talk right then, chances are she wouldn't get his full attention.

- **Find a place with few distractions for important conversations.**
- **Have conversations when the ADHD partner has medications** in his/her system, rather than before or after they have worn off.
- **Avoid late night conversations** when everyone is tired. Ditto first thing in the morning when you have just woken up. Attempts to connect when partners are really *unable* to focus or connect often lead to deep distress on both partners' parts. One strategy, used by Nancie and Steve, is to halt all crucial conversations at 9 p.m., a time when they can both still function. You will know when that halt time is for you.

In addition to these ideas, here are some that can help you comprehend what is being said better:

- **Be patient.** If your partner doesn't seem to respond as you expect, keeping your cool will help you figure out *why not* faster than getting angry or frustrated (which tends to lead to conversations about why you're always angry). Setting a rule never to be rude to each other helps this.
- **Use learning conversations** for emotionally difficult topics. This is a structured speaker/listener technique designed to keep conversations calm and improve listening and clarity of communication. It is reviewed in *The ADHD Effect on Marriage.*
- **Reiterate what you thought you heard. Ask any questions you have:** "So what you're saying is that I need to look for that note in my email…or are you suggesting I'll find it on Facebook?" The partner being asked should embrace the question or reiteration. A belligerent or frustrated response such as a big sigh or, "I just told you it was in your email! Why don't you listen better?" negates this very useful tool.

- **Recap at the end of a conversation.** "This conversation has really helped. Thanks! As I understand it, we've agreed to..."
- **Use short paragraphs rather than lectures to discuss.** Handing over the floor to your partner allows him to chime in and keeps him engaged. If you both do this, then each of you will get a chance to say all that you want. Plus, every time you switch from speaking to listening, you can check whether or not your partner is hearing what you are trying to say.
- **Practice *listening* while your partner is speaking**, rather than forming a rebuttal in your mind. Don't form your response until you've heard all that your partner is saying in his/her short paragraph. This will help you both stay on track better.
- **Get more sleep.** If either of you is sleep deprived, you aren't bringing your full cognitive abilities to the conversation. We can't emphasize the importance of sleep enough!
- **Pursue treatments that target focus**, such as medication, exercise and better sleep. These can improve the "input" side of memory. Better focus aids both comprehension and memory.
- **Do your best to focus on one important topic per conversation**. It is good to remember that the ADHD partner can become overwhelmed. Therefore, it is important not to overstack the deck. Make a couple of appointments to connect if there is more than one critical issue to discuss.

Remembering Negotiations

Couples who are trying to make difficult decisions, such as whether or not to change jobs, or sell versus fix a car, sometimes engage in negotiations that last quite some time. It is frustrating for both when the ADHD partner has trouble remembering what has already been discussed as they try to pick back up where they left off.

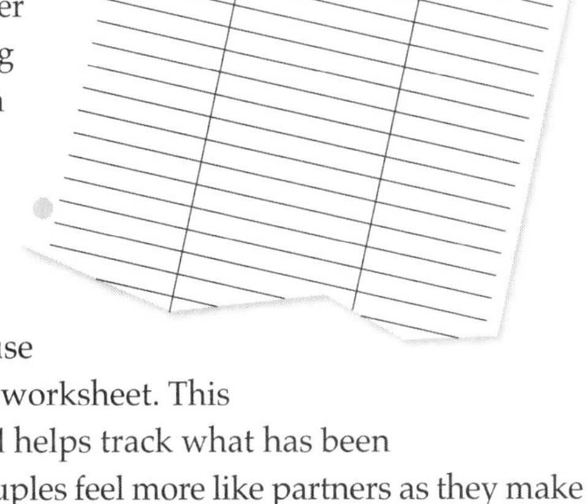

To solve this problem, couples can use a simple three-column worksheet. This deceptively simple tool helps track what has been discussed and helps couples feel more like partners as they make difficult or controversial decisions. To complete it, you should TOGETHER fill in as many ideas as you can in the "reasons to do" column, then together complete the "reasons not to do" column. As you progress, put any creative approaches or ideas into the third column.

HOT SPOT 6
Chronic Lying

Trust and reliability are critical factors in creating stability in a relationship. Lying shreds both. This is why it is so difficult when a partner lies about something really big, such as an affair or using porn, or even a series of small things, such as whether or not the partner left work in time to get home.

> ***ADHD partner:*** *I quit smoking back in April of 2012. About 3 weeks ago, I bought a tin of chewing tobacco. My wife found it and you can imagine the fireworks from there.*

My fault was not telling her what I did because that is a form of lying and/or breaking her trust. This is just an example of what I have done over our 26+ years of marriage. I continue to exercise the definition of insanity—doing the same thing over and over again and expecting a different outcome. I'm having trouble in my mind explaining why I do this, though it often seems to be due to impulsivity. Do you have any suggestions for breaking out of the "little white lies" syndrome that people like me can fall into?

Non-ADHD partner: *My ADHD husband, who is extremely passive aggressive, often lies. I am a calm, patient and caring person and have had many conversations with him about this. Where and how do you set a boundary with someone who copes by lying? My husband struggled as a child and I believe learned to lie in order to protect himself, especially from his ADHD, alcoholic father.*

Some adults with ADHD use "little white lies" to get out of the many difficult situations in which they find themselves, a habit they may have developed in childhood as a way of covering up embarrassment or avoiding a parent, teacher or other authority figure's disappointment or anger. Since not every lie is obvious, the tactic works sometimes in the present moment, but a pattern of lying never works. In fact, just the opposite is true. When a person exhibits a pattern of relying on even small lies, *everything* he or she says becomes suspect, whether or not any particular statement is true.

Within a committed relationship between adults, little white lies are really hard to live with. You are supposed to be partners, with each person able to rely on the other. Chronic lying leaves the partner being lied to in constant doubt. *Is she being truthful this time? How do I know? Do I need to check? How can I verify this? Doesn't he love me? Why would he lie to me if he loves me? Doesn't he trust me? What the hell is going on???* Lying is so destabilizing. It's like a broadside attack on the relationship. This is why it is so infuriating when a partner, caught in the act of a "small" lie responds, "What's the big deal? Who cares if I (...fill in the blank)?" This defensive response misses the entire point—it's not the thing that was lied about that is the problem as much as the *act of lying itself*.

When confronted about lying, ADHD adults tell us over and over again that they use "small" lies for some combination of the following reasons:

- It helps them avoid conflict with their partner in the moment (there are many permutations of this one).
- They are embarrassed by something they did, or by something that happened to them.
- They don't want to disappoint their partner again.
- They are used to doing it—it feels automatic.

We also hear sometimes that they don't have any idea why they lie...they just do.

Let's be clear. Not all people with ADHD chronically lie to cover up symptomatic behaviors. But if this is happening to you, it's a habit that must be broken if you are to thrive. As is the case with so many things in your relationship, it will take the work of you both to develop a new communication pattern.

Let's return to the man who purchased the chewing tobacco and then tried to cover it up. He hid the tin (a form of lying) and when his wife found it, she blew up. Her response reflects two things. First, that his chronic lying (of which he is aware) is really hurting their relationship. Second, that the two of them still have parent/child dynamics in their relationship that need to be addressed. She is acting as an "enforcer" for him—taking on the responsibility for his health management rather than allowing him to be in control. But it is his body, and managing it is his right, even though he may make bad choices at times.

In this case, the husband hid the tobacco for several reasons. He wanted to avoid conflict; he was embarrassed by his impulsivity; and he is used to covering up. What could improve the interaction and help him break his habit?

Just like stopping smoking, moving away from using small lies takes a "safe" environment, new tools, outside support, and positive reinforcement. For this particular couple, it would help them to:

- Make sure the ADHD treatment is optimized to manage "impulsivity" since he has identified this symptom as a particular problem.
- Seek counseling to get assistance with moving away from the parent/child dynamic in which they find themselves. She needs to internalize that even though she doesn't like the tobacco, his health is his business, not hers. In addition, counseling should help them rebalance the power and authority in the relationship.
- Create ways to show her appreciation when he doesn't lie. She might say, "I know that telling me you got that tobacco must have been really hard, and you can guess I'm not that excited, but I really appreciate your being open with me."
- Create a safe way for him to backtrack when he catches himself lying. He ought to be able to go to her and say, "I wasn't completely honest—I just bought some chewing tobacco on impulse and I'm embarrassed." She should, in turn, respond positively to his honesty rather than negatively to the tobacco and the initial impulsivity and lie.
- Use repair methods discussed in this chapter to start to heal the hurts of their past interactions.

So there are many ways to start to reverse the habit of lying. But let's complicate this a little bit more:

> ***ADHD partner:*** *My husband and I both have ADHD. I realize that I am somewhat inattentive, and so at times I forget things that I say, as well as things that he says.*

We can get into conflict when we remember conversations very differently from one another, even if the conversation took place less than an hour before. He claims that I am remembering it all wrong, and that I said things that just sound awful. When I say that I didn't say those things, he tells me I'm lying. It's awful to be thought of as a liar.

In this case, the husband is misinterpreting ADHD symptoms. She is *distracted* and has *poor short-term memory*. What it looks like, at least superficially, is covering up. He thinks she said something that she says she didn't. Like other misinterpretations of symptoms, this one is causing problems that don't need to happen. The solution isn't to distrust her or become angry, but to deal with the symptoms. They might:

- Talk where there are few distractions
- Make sure she is looking him in the eye before speaking
- Jot down some notes
- Get in the habit of recapping what they've heard or agreed to

Another part of the solution is for him to accept that she has trouble remembering and actively seek to listen to her with that mindset, rather than with suspicion. A verbal cue can help support this shift. If he starts to tell her she's lying, she can use a verbal cue to remind him about their agreement that he'll give her the benefit of the doubt. She is not a liar, she has poor memory.

That last interaction is also an example of a "he said/she said" fight, in which their views of what happened in the past directly contradict each other. These are unwinnable arguments, about which we write more in the anger chapter. The important point for now is that couples should *always* stop a "he said/she said" fight and simply start again from wherever they find themselves right at that moment.

As you might suspect, teasing apart symptom misinterpretation from chronic lying takes some effort. And dealing with an ingrained habit of "little white lies" is not very easy. But it is *critically* important. Don't ignore it if you find yourself lying! Trust is broken quickly but takes a long time to rebuild. The reality is that there is no such thing as a little lie in your primary relationship. If your relationship is marred by chronic lying of any sort, then your trust is already broken. It's time to start on the long but very worthwhile road to rebuilding it. We include more on rebuilding trust in Chapter 7 .

HOT SPOT 7
My Partner Acts As If I'm Broken

> **ADHD partner:** *I am the ADHD husband (inattentive type). When we discuss my ADHD issues, my wife usually seems to approach it as if I am the "broken" one in our relationship. I have thoughtfully and slowly read the section on what it is like to be the non-ADHD spouse and more fully feel for how hard it is for my wife. It is hard for me as well since I try so hard. I am using a variety of strategies and tactics but with fewer results than I would like. Question: Is it helpful to point out how difficult it is for me or should I just let my wife come to realize that on her own?*

We frequently hear the word "broken," or undertones of it, and it makes us sad. This woman's ADHD partner is still struggling to manage his ADHD better, but he is also a compassionate, thoughtful partner who is interested in doing right by his wife. He may not be efficient, but he clearly has other very valuable characteristics!

It's all too easy to focus on the weaknesses of your ADHD partner while ignoring your partner's strengths—especially when symptoms are not managed. But thinking of your partner as broken reinforces the negatives of the situation to your mutual detriment.

Think about the difference between saying, "My partner is broken" and "My partner is a good person struggling to find a way to manage difficult ADHD symptoms." The former suggests that the partner is not now, and perhaps never will be, whole. It implies that he is not good or useful in any way. The latter starts with the positive and also credits the partner for his positive motives—which would certainly be appropriate in the case of the man with ADHD above.

When you think your partner is broken, you try to fix your partner. When you think your partner is whole but struggling with a huge challenge, you support him. By now you probably can figure out which approach works better to achieve the goal you want—a strong, happy, thriving relationship.

Communication Ideas to Think About–Again and Again

- You're more different than you realize. Make no assumptions about your partner's motivations. Respect your partner's way of being in the world.
- Don't fall into these common traps: Non-ADHD is better/right; "ADHD" means "broken." Both of you will suffer from such thinking.
- Make creating attend time one of your very top priorities!
- Fight good fights.
- Use verbal cues to calm your relationship.
- Be generous at offering and accepting repair attempts. Learn to use repair attempts during the heat of an argument to de-escalate it.

- Avoid acting like your partner's parent. Rebalance the power in your relationship (see Chapter 6).
- Forgive and validate your partner. This will help you both feel better about your relationship.
- Stop thinking about solving problems—for most of them, you'll be creating negotiated work-arounds instead.
- Lying destroys trust. Eradicate lying from your relationship and make it safe to be honest about problems.
- Don't take your partner's ADHD symptoms personally.

Can't You Just Lighten Up? Anger in Your Relationship

"I cannot say whether things will get better if they change; what I can say is they must change if they are to get better."

— Georg Christoph Lichtenberg

You will each experience a swirl of emotions as you work to change your relationship. Up, down...hopeful, depressed... thrilled, angry...and progress is probably slower than you might wish it to be. One reason for the slow progress may well be anger. In ADHD-impacted relationships, anger is common, difficult to manage, and often needlessly damaging.

Everyone gets angry, and this is a good thing. It is an important emotion that tells us that we need to change our current direction or interaction. Even in a very healthy relationship, you will still—sometimes—feel anger. So we are *not* suggesting that your goal should be to eliminate anger, though you will do better if you eliminate a few specific *types* of anger that are always damaging. What we would like is to help you get to the point where love and happiness are *enough of a norm* to satisfy both partners, while anger is the exception.

Every couple has a different set point for how much anger they can handle. Some couples view "bickering" as constructive disagreement, for example, while others cannot tolerate it at all. Furthermore, anger is a complex emotion in primary relationships. It has multiple potential sources and is used both defensively and aggressively. There's chronic anger that one might describe as "mad all the time." This type of anger works like a filter through which the angry person sees all activities and interactions. Nothing your partner says or does is good enough, and even the most innocuous statement is seen as an insult or negative. This is a difficult anger to see if you are the one who has it. You know you are "cranky" and that you don't particularly like the way your days are going, but you probably feel justified in your anger and may blame what's going on around you, or the person you are with, for your "bad mood."

Anger can also be used as a tool to wield power. Bullying is a good example of this, as is anger that is targeted at a partner as punishment or warning to get him to change his ways.

And there is physiologically based anger—a quick trigger variety that explodes unexpectedly due to lack of impulse control, too much testosterone, PMS or some other chemical issue.

One of the most common varieties of anger that we see results from a long series of repetitive interactions between partners, leading to feelings of being overwhelmed for one or both of them. This particular anger may result in getting "flooded" by emotion, leading to hurtful, out-of-control fights.

We hope to help you assess the potential sources of your own anger and then, once you have a better understanding, test some of the anger-busting techniques we suggest to see if they work for you. Be aware that successful strategies are not always intuitive and may not be the first response that comes to mind.

We also review angry communication in Chapter 3. How you express yourselves during a fight—and repair from it—is critical (pun intended!) to the health of your relationship. So if you skipped immediately to this chapter, please backtrack and read that one, too!

HOTSPOT 8
Anger and Grief—Feeling Duped

Adult ADHD is still wildly underdiagnosed, and a majority of today's adults with ADHD came into their relationships unaware of their ADHD. Though some couples sail along just fine with undiagnosed ADHD in their relationship, most don't, and by the time they find a counselor they are typically in real trouble and can be very angry at each other. Some non-ADHD partners feel duped by their partner and his or her ADHD.

> **Non-ADHD partner:** *I'm angry at myself. I decided to marry my husband because he possessed what I most wanted in a life partner. He was spontaneous, energetic, loving and kind. He protected me, cherished me, was always there for me and held me up on a pedestal for the first time in my life. Now I feel cheated, lied to and sold a bill of goods. When I read there was such a thing as a hyperfocused courtship, I just started bawling. It was all a great big deception. This is not what I signed up for at all. I am having a hard time forgiving this FUNDAMENTAL deception and trying to sort through what the bare minimum I can accept is. All the characteristics I "had to have" in a life partner include reliability, honesty, patience, and support. I have NONE OF THIS. I have an angry man, around whom I walk on eggshells. He tears me down at every opportunity, yells at me and the kids, and cannot have a discussion or reach a compromise on any issue without getting defensive and storming off. He is stubborn, dismissive and can't hear anyone else.*

What's Hyperfocus Courtship?

All adults experience significant increases in the "attention" neurotransmitter dopamine while infatuated. This allows adults with ADHD to be unusually attentive to, or *hyperfocused* upon, their partner during courtship. Over time, the dopamine increase of infatuation goes away, and the ADHD partner returns to a more normal, low-dopamine, low-attention state. This shift to being more ADHD symptomatic is often a shock to the relationship.

This woman sees great differences between the man who courted her and the man she experiences daily in her marriage. She is angry because, in her eyes, he deceived her in the most fundamental way—"lying" to her about who he really is with his courtship behavior. She has heard about "hyperfocus courtship," yet she has failed to understand a key point. This is not something her husband *did to her* intentionally, nor was it something of which he was aware. All he knew was how good it felt to be with her. Hyperfocus courtship stems from a chemical boost biologically selected over millennia to get people together, and it's no more *deceptive* than the chemical boost mothers get after giving birth that connects them with their babies. (If we didn't get this "high," might we consider just rolling over and not feeding the baby at 1 a.m.?)

We don't endorse this husband's behavior. His aggressiveness, defensiveness, stubbornness, and willingness to dismiss those around him are all known predictors of divorce. His ADHD is out of control, as are his behaviors. But regardless of his terrible behaviors, we must point out that this woman's anger adds to the hurt for herself and her relationship. The issue for this couple isn't the past—it's the present. As long as she nurtures anger and resentment about his past "fundamental deception" and, importantly, reinforces her anger at herself, it will be hard for her to move forward positively to create change or feel good about herself. She needs to step back, acknowledge that her blame has been misplaced, and start focusing on what their mutual next steps are based upon where they are today.

> **Non-ADHD partner:** *We've been married a very long time. Seven years into our marriage and after two kids, we separated. I flourished in the separation, but that's when my husband began courting me in earnest. I so wanted my two children to have their parents together and I really hoped it would work out, so we got back together even though my gut told me to run the other way. In all the years since, we have continued to flirt with separation as we struggled.*
>
> *About 15 years ago, I gave my husband some literature on ADHD and asked that he get tested. He was scared to do so, but did. It turns out that he's the poster boy for ADHD. He is well loved by all who know him. He has a bigger than life persona and lacks any filter. But at home he is not that guy. He is always telling me that if I could just be happy, we could be so happy. Every new try to be happy gives me a set of expectations, and when I fail, he withdraws his affection—sometimes for 1-3 years at a time! When this happens, I feel it must be me. What man would not want or need any affection or intimacy for years at a time?*
>
> *He has read your book and was very affected by the impact that ADHD can have on a spouse, but I'm ready to move on. At this point I am so angry and sad about all the lost years that all I do is cry. My husband feels so bad, and I don't want to hurt him, but the anger is consuming me. I feel I was cheated out of things I cannot get back. Can you help me get past this?*

This woman has been unhappily married for so long that she grieves the loss of her *life*. For non-ADHD partners who have struggled for decades, this grief is all too common, and hers is intensified by the fact that she got separated, liked it, and chose to come back. She had a chance for a different life, but she gave it up.

It's likely that her sadness, now that it is out in the open, feels completely overwhelming to her husband who, with new information, now sees more clearly the connection between his ADHD symptoms and her troubled life. Yet, in spite of her husband feeling overwhelmed, her ability to cry these tears and feel this grief is a *good* thing. It's been there all along, but until now she could not give it a name and context that they could both understand. It's no longer a matter of his saying to her, "Just be happier." He now understands why that approach hasn't worked and has the chance to appropriately address his symptomatic behaviors that initiate their symptom/response/response interactions. She needs lots of empathy and hugs from him as well as therapy to work through her grief, and he needs some really good professional help to get him to a completely new place with his ADHD. Perhaps a combination of psychiatrist, coach, physical exercise and mindfulness training will move him along as quickly as the situation warrants.

As she deals with her grief, she should also recognize that it stems from her own behavior as well as her husband's. She cannot blame him for the fact that she chose to put her family's togetherness ahead of her gut instinct to leave the marriage. As tempting as it is to just blame the ADHD, the problem is often more complex than that. Grief is the result of decisions made by both partners: an ADHD partner doesn't address his symptoms soon enough, or a non-ADHD partner moves into parenting behavior and takes on too many responsibilities or simply decides to put family first. In order to succeed in healing the relationship, both partners need to examine their individual behavior and decisions and conscientiously move forward in ways that support their partner and themselves.

When Do I Give Up?

Here's our final example of feeling duped:

> **Non-ADHD partner:** *My anger has turned to sadness. I feel sad and disappointed that my life has turned out this way and that my partner and I have to deal with the way he is wired, something that has diminished his effectiveness, efficiency and his ability to use his very powerful brain. I know I'm supposed to be focusing on the strengths-based approach, but I'm just not feeling it. I feel cheated. I live with daily stress that I constantly work to minimize. Our financial resources have been negatively impacted by my partner's ADHD. How does one reconcile the insidious, long-range anger, sadness and stress? When does it make sense to seriously consider the question of whether I want to live this way for the rest of my life?*

How many of us have secretly wondered, *What if I didn't have ADHD?* or *What would it be like if I were married to someone who didn't have ADHD?* For many, it's an easy leap to ask whether or not you wish to live like this for the rest of your life.

As Garrison Keilor memorably said in a performance Melissa attended recently, "Marriage is tough. It's hard living with your most well-informed critic." Creating a relationship in which both individuals feel fulfilled, heard and loved is a real challenge, and having ADHD symptoms in the mix makes it harder for many couples.

Questions about whether or not to stay can best be answered, we think, when couples know they have done their utmost to bring their best selves to their relationship. It takes time to explore how to bring your best self forward. Couples facing ADHD issues must learn to optimize treatment, set better boundaries, learn new communication techniques, and more. But at some point couples know inside themselves that they are ready to ask *is our "best" still a good fit? Can we find joy and happiness from what we each contribute to our partnership? Can we love ourselves, and our partners, for all the wonderful things they present… as well as their flaws?*

We urge couples to give themselves enough time to fully understand how ADHD impacts them and what their options are in dealing with it. Not all couples succeed in turning their relationship around, but it's amazing how many do.

Couples sometimes ask how long this process will take, and, of course, the answer to that question varies greatly. In general, though, we see that *once the ADHD partner fully understands the issues that ADHD symptoms contribute to the relationship and initiates a concerted attempt to optimize treatment,* it takes at least 6-18 months of serious effort on the part of both partners to turn things around. The fastest turnaround Melissa has seen took three months and, of course, there are couples who simply don't find success. If the ADHD partner does not participate, then the symptom/response/ response pattern is hard to interrupt, and typically the couple finds that they continue to struggle until one of them gives up. If the non-ADHD partner does not participate, then that crucial first negative response to ADHD symptoms also extends their conflict. Nancie has seen unfortunate results when, in one case, a non-ADHD partner did not give her ADHD partner enough time to put into practice the skills and awareness he was receiving in counseling and coaching. Patience, in these circumstances, is a critical virtue.

So don't be surprised or offended if you or your partner is asking, "Can we really do this?" and "Can we hang in there?" These are natural, and we think healthy, questions to ask given your struggles. The answer, we hope, is yes. But if you find that your best selves are no longer a good match, or that one party is unable to locate and act on their inner caring, loving, supportive self even given adequate tools and time, then it may be time for a new path.

HOT SPOT 9
Nothing Ever Seems to Change

ADHD symptomatic behaviors are often pervasive and repetitive. Medication can help improve focus, clarity, impulse control and more, but changing lifelong habits and behaviors is a lengthy and arduous process. "Pills don't teach skills" is what some say, yet it's the skills (i.e., behaviors) that are *all important* in a relationship. If you have focus but don't apply that focus to your relationship, it may well collapse. Practicing a new skill is hard work but really, really worth the effort. The payoff—a balanced relationship in which each of you can be loved for who you are and what you contribute—is huge.

But first, you must get past those pervasive and annoyingly repetitive symptoms! Well, "annoying" is too soft a word. The repetitive nature of ADHD underpins a good part of the anger seen in so many ADHD-impacted relationships. A typical pattern starts with one or more symptoms that encourage the non-ADHD partner to respond with anger. This anger usually develops over time in response to the new burdens placed upon him or her by ADHD symptoms. The pattern of interaction escalates when the ADHD partner responds to the anger of the non-ADHD partner rather than the original concern. It's classic symptom / response / response.

It's important for ADHD spouses to hear this: symptoms have a *tremendous* impact on *non*-ADHD and other-ADHD partners. Every. Single. Day. These partners have too large a share of your joint responsibilities. They don't know what their ADHD partner is going to do next. They don't understand why their partner won't "try harder" or can't accomplish things that seem easy to the non-ADHD partner. They are *victims* of distraction, tardiness, impulsive anger and impulsive financial decisions.

Perhaps most frustrating of all, this is often the first time in their lives that they cannot, somehow, figure out how to "fix" it. They will certainly try—and you've seen this in your household—but the reality is that at the very bottom of the symptom / response / response pattern is a *symptom*. Non-ADHD partners have very little control over what's happening to them. They *cannot* fix ADHD symptoms because they aren't theirs to fix.

It's incredibly frustrating. And because they've never experienced something like this before, they don't comprehend why their partner isn't more responsive! This is particularly the case if ADHD was not diagnosed until well into the marriage. We work with non-ADHD partners who secretly think that if they had ADHD, *they* would be able to whip those symptoms into place, lickety-split! They would just create a plan of attack and execute it! Of course, that's a very *non-ADHD* approach. It doesn't take into account the idea that their partner would do exactly the same thing if he or she could. No one wants to lose a job, disappoint a spouse, always be late, forget to pay the electric bill, feel like a failure, or have difficulty controlling emotions! If "fixing" ADHD were easy *for someone who has ADHD*, it would already have happened!

So, because it's always worked for *them*, non-ADHD partners push for change. They plan. They make suggestions. They try things. When symptoms keep coming back, they try some more. Eventually, they get frustrated and angry at their lack of success and try to take more control. ADHD partners don't appreciate this, and their fights escalate. Eventually the fights are regular, the anger colors everything, nobody trusts anybody anymore, and both feel overwhelmed.

> **Non-ADHD partner:** *Two weeks ago I was doing errands and called my husband to see if he would be ready to go out when I returned. He told me he was in the middle of getting ready, but when I returned home my husband had not moved to get ready at all. He was still unshaven and in PJs—and he*

> *was on the phone with tech support for his computer. I felt so powerless, helpless, and angry that I slammed my arm into the door. I felt in that moment that I could kill my husband. Rage. Anger. Fury. Frustration. This type of thing happened three times that week. Another time he forgot to pick me up from the airport. Of course, I found out two weeks later that he was out of medication, and amazingly, that didn't seem to worry him. I, however, am at my wit's end.*

This woman wants to be able to rely on her husband. Instead, she gets "little white lies" and distracted behavior. And to top it off, he's not concerned about forgetting to get more medication that might help him improve. Her response? Rage and fury. This has happened many times before, and his lack of concern suggests that it's going to continue to happen.

Her fury is triggered because she feels boxed in. Her partner is in denial about the impact of his ADHD, and she finds herself in a "no win" situation. Until her partner determines it's important to be on top of his ADHD *at all times* and starts interacting with her more productively, she is stuck. Their relationship will not improve. Without his more active participation, she has only three real choices…and all of them are bad:

1. Improve her situation by *leaving* the relationship.
2. *Adapt* her behavior to his ADHD symptoms, thus giving up on her own life and needs. As this will inevitably lead to resentment and anger, it's not a sustainable or healthy option for either party.
3. *Fight back,* which may well increase discord and hostility in the relationship (see the communications chapter for how to push back without damage).

The only way out of this dilemma is for the ADHD partner to add a fourth choice for his wife: he can choose to manage his ADHD better. That would allow his wife to respond positively to his changes and symptom management, which she would really like to do. Together (but only together) they can thrust the relationship in a new direction. But to start this interaction, he must put a full court press on treating the ADHD symptoms. A continuation of his "don't worry/be happy" attitude towards his treatment will result in either a chronically unhappy and negative relationship with his partner or divorce. Because of her limited options, he can either move out of denial and set the structures in place to become *reliable enough* with his wife, or he can suffer significant consequences. You might think that the consequence of her fury would make the need for change obvious. Unfortunately, this is often not the case.

"Consequences" and ADHD

Non-ADHD partners who try to let the consequences of an ADHD partner's actions inspire change are often confounded by what seems to be a stubborn refusal to address obvious problems.

> ***Non-ADHD partner:*** *Between ADHD and Bi-Polar Disorder, my husband goes through "cycles." It starts with a period of 2-4 days where he is on top of everything, pleasant, very well aware of his issues and does what he can to minimize his impact on everyone. But then he changes. For example, this past week after a long car drive and being cooped up, as well as questionable coverage on his medications, he became incredibly distracted, "staticky" and conflict-seeking. While I understand his issues, this repetitious cycle of start and stop has created so much anger and resentment for the burden I am forced to carry on my shoulders. I realize that sometimes you have to let people face natural consequences and the like for their actions, but every consequence generally impacts me and our two kids one way or another. How do I continue to stay supportive and tolerant when these cycles seem to have no end?*

Notice her comment: "I realize that sometimes you have to let people face natural consequences and the like for their actions." She believes that facing consequences will change her husband's behavior. This idea is one that many therapists teach couples. But does it work? Will someone with ADHD change his behavior based on the natural consequences of his actions? ADHD expert Russell Barkley thinks that consequences aren't the issue—acting on intentions at the right time is. He notes in his book *Taking Charge of Adult ADHD*, "The problems that ADHD creates for you have more to do with not using what you know at critical points of performance in your life than with not knowing what to do."

Our experience would suggest that short of an all-out disaster, by the time a person with ADHD is an adult, *she has already adapted to her own ADHD symptoms and consequences*. We do not suggest the adaptations are healthy or in her best interests, only that we observe that many adults with ADHD have developed a very high personal pain threshold as a coping mechanism for dealing with what was, until very recently, a life of undiagnosed ADHD. If you cannot explain your behaviors because you don't know about the ADHD, you learn to let go of things that you cannot control—and at least *act* as if they don't bother you.

This has implications. Non-ADHD partners cannot successfully "parent" ADHD partners. On the other hand, they cannot wait for the consequences of having ADHD to just "sink in" when the threshold for pain is so high. Most ADHD partners have been having problems for a long time and, for most of them, the consequences of those problems haven't created change yet. It takes a true crisis for pain to lead to action. The result is that non-ADHD partners must find a way to *lobby* effectively for what they want, while also respecting the authority of the person with ADHD to live her life as she chooses. In other words, the best option for non-ADHD partners is to understand their very limited power to create change in their partner but to continue to *lobby* for change even though lobbying does not guarantee change.

For those of you with ADHD, please hear what we are saying. Your tolerance for pain and failure—the ability to "go with the flow"—is most likely a *coping strategy* for dealing with the inconsistencies that your ADHD has created. It is time for a new coping strategy. The old one—creating a high pain threshold and going along—has not served you as well as you have convinced yourself. It is part of the reason that your relationship is in trouble. That pain threshold does not align with your partner's needs. A better relationship strategy is to face the ADHD symptoms head on and treat them, using every resource science suggests will work.

HOT SPOT 10
My Partner Ignores My Unhappiness

Too many ADHD and non-ADHD partners deny the validity—sometimes the very existence—of their partner's unhappiness and pain. We have something we want all of you to hear. ADHD doesn't cause divorce—denial does. With good treatment and effort, ADHD is highly manageable for most people. Bad attitudes and denial in either partner, however, are not.

> **Non-ADHD partner:** *Here are some examples of what I hear from my husband with ADHD: "You started it, so I snapped at you. So what? Get over it. You are too sensitive." When he snaps at me or cuts me off, I admittedly go ballistic because I don't know what else to do. He claims I take it to a whole new level and that I have a "mean streak" in me because anyone who claims to love someone wouldn't freak out on him like that. "The punishment never matches the crime," he says. He thinks I should let him snap/bark at me and it would be over in two seconds. It might be over for him, but he*

doesn't realize the effect and inner turmoil it has on me. He doesn't even seem to care when I tell him how hurt I am.

I've told him to just apologize when he hurts my feelings or is harsh or shuts me down. He is incredibly impatient with me and he knows it. He says, "I'm impatient with everyone." I've gone so far as to say it's okay to bark at me if he says he's sorry afterwards. But he refuses. He says "I'm not going to go through my life apologizing, and besides, it's just words." So I tell him he has two choices: he can apologize or he can receive my "wrath," which is me going ballistic. He doesn't like either choice. He says, "Just bark back." It's a disconnect. I don't want to "bark back." He doesn't seem to care at all that what he does affects or hurts me. And when I cry, he says, "Oh my God, are you going to cry now?" I don't know how much more of the insensitivity I can take. He says to me, "Just be nice," and I say, "I'll be nice to you if you are nice to me." His response is "why does it always have to start with me? Do you ever work on yourself?" I'm extremely frustrated.

This comment demonstrates a very common sort of mutual denial. The husband has decided he doesn't need to be a good partner. He justifies his poor behavior. He's "impatient with everyone," and she is always "freaking out" in ways that he feels are inappropriate. She, for her part, justifies her ballistic responses ("What else can I do?") and blames him for her responses. They have gotten into a very negative downward spiral—a tit-for-tat, you-go-first dance. Each partner's refusal to hear the other's request to stand down drives them further apart and makes them feel more overwhelmed.

Notice how the ADHD partner is using his ADHD symptoms (in this case, lack of impulse control) as an excuse for continued poor behavior. He argues that it's okay to be impatient (and presumably mean) because he always has been.

He can move past a blow-up immediately (because of his ADHD "now and not now" time zones) and, therefore, she must, too.

Though it is tempting to blame the ADHD partner in this case, he is not the only person creating problems. "Going ballistic" is never constructive behavior, and this is easy to see from outside this relationship looking in. It's probably harder for her to see when faced with his logic that it's okay to be impatient and rude. She is trying to manipulate his behavior by setting up two choices for him—"apologize or risk my wrath." He's having none of that. His interpretation of her two choices seems to be that she wants him to grovel, apologize and be dominated.

This couple would likely benefit from professional help if they would seek it. Each partner needs to stop blaming the other and take personal responsibility for his or her own poor behavior. Impulsivity should be added to his target symptom list, and he should consider trying medications and other treatment strategies that might help him control it. She needs to learn how to engage in "good fights." Both would likely benefit from therapeutic introspection as well as discussing tactics for positive interactions. There is a path out of their mess, but right now they are simply locked in a battle of mutual denial and blame.

HOT SPOT 11
Overwhelmed with Anger—Flooding

Anger can be a difficult emotion to manage, and at no time is it harder to deal with than when one or both partners become flooded with overwhelming emotions. You've probably had "flooded" arguments—these are the times when you know you should disengage but you just *can't!* You have to fight to win or survive and no other outcome feels possible.

What is Flooding?

Flooding is a physiological response we have when we feel in danger or become extremely emotional. The parts of our brain needed to fight back are *flooded* with blood and oxygen for better performance. Unfortunately, these are taken from the parts of the brain that deal with logical thinking. When you are flooded you might sense you shouldn't keep fighting, but you can't seem to get the logical part of your brain to actually get you to stop. It's not fully functioning.

Couples describe flooding like this:

Couple #1—ADHD partner: *I fully acknowledge that I do NOT want to argue with my wife anymore. However, when discussing something with my spouse, I still sometimes have an overwhelming sense of being attacked, of being bossed around, and of being talked down to, and these feelings are greatly increased if this happens in front of the kids. What can I do to help ease these feelings so that I don't act out impulsively and hurtfully towards my wife? I don't want to do this, but it is very hard to control these emotions.*

Couple #2—Non-ADHD partner: *How do you react to a total anger meltdown? Talking is not an option; I can leave or stay, but neither helps.*

Couple #3—ADHD partner: *A common scenario with my ADHD wife goes something like this: I do something that triggers a reaction on her part. Then, it doesn't seem to matter much what it is that I do—and her response to my subsequent actions always surprises me.*

If I try to say anything in response to her reaction—whether it be defensive (as is my "natural" reaction when I'm under attack, though I've been learning to control this and not get defensive) or empathetic ("Sorry about that... can I do anything for you right now?")—it tends to get interpreted as further evidence of whatever it is she saw in my original action. This makes her angrier with me. So sometimes, no matter what I say/do, she will just get angrier and more aggressive (verbally, emotionally, sometimes physically). If I withdraw, that triggers even more anger. Once we've gone over that cliff, nothing I do is okay. All I can do is try to minimize the symptom/response/response pattern and wait it out.

The first step in managing flooding is to recognize it for what it is—a physiological state from which it is very hard to exit, and in which it is impossible to create anything constructive. Flooding never helps. It is an anger state that is simply to be avoided, and the only way to do that is to stop it before it starts. In the chapter on communication, you will find instructions for setting and using verbal cues that are a great tool for stopping arguments before they get to the flooded stage.

These couples' descriptions also contain the seeds of other ideas for how to avoid flooding. The first man identifies a specific situation in which he is more likely to be flooded—when attacked in front of his children. His wife *loses* him if she criticizes him in front of the kids because he expends his energy on the task of not getting flooded and lashing out. This is constructive, as he doesn't wish to hurt his partner. But it means that he is not focused on what she is saying. Her efforts will, therefore, be in vain. So one tool for this couple would be for the wife to understand that she is working against herself if she doesn't exert more self-control. She needs to find better times, and more constructive ways, to approach him.

The second and third couples have a different issue. The overwhelmed partner simply loses control. The way to address this isn't during the confrontation—the writers acknowledge this directly by pointing out that nothing the couple does at these times matters. They need to pick another time, probably in the presence of a counselor, to talk about anger management issues. *Could this be a side effect of medication, or has it been a lifelong problem? Can it be treated somehow? Are there identifiable triggers, such as specific topics or times of day? Are there family of origin issues? Is the diagnosis right?* These couples need to agree that the anger is harmful to them both and be detectives about how to impact and change the behavior. But they can't change any of it during the flooded fury. There is no "logical" part of the brain available to "talk."

Flooding can lead to physical abuse, as suggested in the third couple's quote. There is an entire body of literature and therapy about spousal abuse that we do not have the space to get into here. However, if your relationship has become physically abusive, we strongly suggest seeking professional help immediately. An expert can help you ascertain the safest way to change or end the relationship. *Do not* agree to just go along with this one—your safety is too important!

Verbal Abuse, Impulsive Anger, and the Hothead

That last couple referenced both physical and verbal abuse. Physical violence is obvious and should not be tolerated in any relationship. Unfortunately, many are more casual about verbal abuse.

> **Non-ADHD partner:** *My ADHD spouse's bursts of anger have risen, in my mind, to the point of verbal abuse. I restrict my behavior and think about how to behave in order to keep him from getting angry. You've said that you can't control the other person's anger, but I honestly don't know how else to behave except to try to avoid setting him off. His outbursts are very upsetting to me, and I try very hard to avoid causing them. If I tell him his anger bothers me, he often apologizes after the fact, but it's become such a pattern that it's hard to accept his apology as sincere. In a nutshell, I feel like I'm in an abusive relationship.*

Verbal abuse is too common when couples are chronically and deeply angry with each other. And it's not just impulsive ADHD spouses, such as the man in this example, who abuse. Melissa admits that she fell into a pattern of verbal abuse for a period of time in her relationship. Her justification at the time was that she felt out of control and overwhelmed by her husband's unwillingness to even consider his role in their marriage issues. Because she was frustrated beyond measure, she responded by first picking on him, then escalating to belittling and verbally attacking him. But there is *no* justification for this behavior. It's simply not part of a healthy relationship.

When you hear the words "verbal abuse," you probably don't think of yourself as a perpetrator. Melissa certainly didn't. Yet step away from your justifications and reasons for a moment, and simply listen to the actual words and delivery. You may be shocked to discover that you are an abuser. Verbal bullying, hurtful name-calling, and belittling are obviously abusive. Harassing, trivializing, berating, blaming and even defining someone else in a negative way can also be considered abusive. We urge everyone who reads this book to look carefully at their interactions for the next two weeks and ask the question *Are my words abusive?*

No amount of frustration, defensiveness, or lack of impulse control justifies verbal abuse. If you or your spouse is being abusive, this needs to stop immediately. If you can't manage to set new rules for yourself to stop abusing your partner, then seek the help of a professional counselor.

Physiological and Chemical Anger

Impulsive anger is one variety of anger that can have physiological roots. Others include hormonal anger and head trauma. If you have anger issues, it may make sense to talk with your doctor about whether or not there could be a physiological basis to your anger that might be managed, at least in part, with medicinal or therapeutic intervention.

Impulsive anger can also be impacted by the medications used to treat ADHD.On the positive side, some ADHD medications can improve your ability to "stop and think," which can allow you to consider whether the angry thing you are about to say is a good idea. On the other side of the scale, some medications increase irritability in some people. You should note, and report to your doctor, any changes in mood that you feel when you take a new medication so that the change can be assessed against your treatment goals. If you start an amphetamine, for example, and suddenly become more focused but extremely touchy, that's not a good outcome! You and your doctor will want to consider a lower dose or, perhaps, a completely different medication to deal with that side effect.

HOT SPOT 12
The Anger Filter

We all see the world through a lens of interpretation based upon our experiences, our backgrounds, and our basic personality characteristics such as optimism or pessimism. When couples struggle, it is common that one or both of them develops a lens of negativity. Life is genuinely hard, and ADHD and responses to ADHD wear both partners down. After a while, one or both starts to think *here it comes again. I can't take this!* Nancie and Melissa call this the anger filter. All information and actions are interpreted through a veil of anger or frustration, perhaps even a feeling that *I've reached the end of my rope.*

This negative filter is contagious. Once one person has it, the chances seem to increase that the other will also develop it. After all, if your partner *never gives you a break, or never seems to deal with his/her issues,* what is there to be optimistic about? Nothing will ever change….bleh!

The Importance of Internal Stories

The anger filter is connected to the internal stories that individuals tell themselves. It's not surprising that non-ADHD partners develop a negative filter when they feel neglected and repeatedly observe an ADHD partner's struggle to pay attention or complete a "simple" task. The internal story reads, *This problem isn't ending, and I'm going to be dealing with it forever…I don't know if I can handle that—Oh no!*

It's also not surprising when an ADHD partner develops an angry or negative filter. Many have faced huge hurdles and disapproval during their lives, and if they didn't before, they are facing them now with the added pressures of marriage and (often) children. Their partners are cranky (or worse), and the ADHD symptoms typically are a huge area of contention. Their internal story may go something like this: *No one ever gives me a break, and folks need to lighten up. If my partner weren't so mad all the time and would just support me, my difficult life would be so much easier!*

Both of these internal stories are self-perpetuating. The more you tell yourself the story, the more negative your filter becomes. As you evaluate interactions through the deepening filter, even the most innocuous events seem to reinforce the story. The filter makes the story "true" in your mind, even if it isn't true in reality.

You may be puzzled as you read this. Perhaps you are thinking: *It's not a filter…my partner is genuinely mad and blames me all the time.* Maybe. Or maybe not. Here's an example of a subtle negative filter that is causing trouble for one couple:

> **Non-ADHD partner:** *Because of our different ways of thinking and because of a lack of detail in things my husband asks of me, I find I must ask questions to fully understand what he is requesting. Now that we are aware of ADHD in the relationship, he interprets my questions as an accusation that he can't think things through or explain adequately. Now that I know more about ADHD, his response to my*

questioning makes more sense to me, but how do we get past this roadblock?

This man's internal story may be this: *since I have ADHD, she's blaming me for all of our problems. That's not fair!* He has developed a negative lens through which he interprets her genuine efforts to understand what he is saying. Imagine how different his response would be if his filter were more positive: *Wow! My wife is so interested in what I'm saying that she wants to know more!*

Melissa and her husband used to have a very similar type of issue. George is a brilliant man, whose mind races and who connects ideas with great facility and in surprising ways (one of his ADHD strengths, perhaps!) When he is talking, he sometimes thinks about something in his head that is pertinent to what he is saying, but the idea goes by so quickly that he doesn't actually verbalize it. Melissa, however, gets lost because his words have "skipped" a step in his logic flow. She used to ask questions to clarify his meaning, but this really annoyed George. He would become impatient and cut Melissa off or respond in ways that suggested he thought her questions were stupid. His responses made her very angry—she felt she deserved a respectful response. Over time, George developed a negative internal story: *she rarely understands what I'm saying, and we often fight when I share things…it's a hassle to talk to her.* Acting on that internal story, he stopped including her in his interests as often. This disengagement, of course, did nothing to strengthen their bonds.

Over time, they figured out what was really going on and were able to start to laugh about it. George's quick mind became recognized for the plus that it is, and his skipping over key details became a quirk to which they could constructively respond. Melissa would laugh and say, "I think you've missed a step there!" and George could then backtrack and fill her in. He started to view their conversations through a different lens: *she's interested in what I have to say but is having trouble following my logic.* That's far more neutral, and it encouraged both conversation and the strengthening of their bonds. It's just one demonstration of how changing one's internal story can radically alter one's feelings and interactions.

Many internal stories impact our behavior towards our partner. But when ADHD goes undiagnosed for a long time, many of these stories are negative. One of the most important lenses that needs to be identified and changed if you are going to thrive is the one in Hot Spot 2:

Things are never going to change!

For the vast majority of couples impacted by ADHD *who genuinely decide to really own and address both the ADHD and the responses to the ADHD*, this story simply is not true! ADHD can be managed most of the time, and responses can be changed dramatically, just as Melissa and George changed their responses to how they interacted when his mind moved too quickly.

Yet the "things will never change" story is pernicious. Even as couples see improvement, small setbacks can trigger a fear response, such as *Oh no! This means we're going back to the bad old days!* Ironically, that very response increases the chances that this will become true, since it results in anxiety that can demotivate both partners or causes them to react defensively or angrily. Remember, it takes a lot of effort to manage ADHD. Together, you will experience many failures as you both try to improve things. That's a good thing. You can learn from those failures.

So don't fall victim to the "things will never change" internal story. Remain positive and enthusiastic, instead. Things didn't change in the past because you didn't understand the impact of ADHD symptom / response / response, and you didn't have the tools to help. Now you do. Do yourselves the huge favor of internalizing that news. Change your story to the more positive thought that *this will take time and effort but others have done it and we can, too!*

Things *Can* Change–An Example of How to Do It

Let us be very, very clear. We are NOT in ANY WAY saying that the problems caused by ADHD are simply problems created by the stories you tell yourself. That would be tremendously insulting as well as factually incorrect. ADHD symptoms are real and physiologically based. What we are trying to communicate is that the stories you carry inside you—those lenses through which you interpret your daily life—make a huge difference when it comes to living with ADHD. We're not encouraging you to *make up* stories to mask ADHD or responses to it. We're suggesting that you give each other the benefit of the doubt—perhaps longer than you might think prudent—in order to let the ADHD partner have enough time to figure out just how to manage his or her symptoms. This allows you to remain partners, rather than adversaries. It's not easy, and making changes always takes more time than you want it to. Furthermore, it's often very emotionally complex.

> ***Non-ADHD partner:*** *We wanted to set up a new bed routine, so we agreed he would come to bed because he needed more sleep to manage his ADHD symptoms. I asked him if he intended to do so that night. He said yes, he was coming up soon, but an hour later I went downstairs and he was watching the game with one of our kids. I was so furious! What do I do in those cases?*

This bedtime story is an incredibly common one. In fact, we are betting that everyone who reads this book has had a very similar experience. This couple made an agreement. The ADHD partner confirmed that he was on board with that agreement. But then he didn't follow through. After about an hour of increasing anxiety that her husband wasn't upstairs, which turned into dread and anger *(not again!)* she finally came downstairs to find him watching the game with one of their kids.

She could not control her disappointment and anger. Maybe she was angry because she spent half an hour of precious time with her husband talking about this issue and creating an approach—time that seemed wasted now. Or maybe she was angry at the unfairness of ADHD symptoms—she didn't sign on for this sort of hassle! Perhaps she was angry at her husband for not working hard enough to do better—or angry at herself for allowing herself to hope this might improve things, only to see her hopes dashed...again.

He, for his part, probably experienced a mixture of emotions in response to her fury. Guilt or embarrassment—yes, he agreed and then didn't follow through. Anger at this and other responses she has towards him—it seems like she's always angry or disappointed. Ambivalence—he really wants to make this relationship work, but she is not the person he thought he was marrying...and he's not sure he really wants to go to bed with her when she's like that—watching the game would be much more fun! Plus she's acting like his mom again by checking up on him, which is insulting. Perhaps he feels remorse or self-pity—he understands logically that he would benefit from more sleep...but getting himself to do these things is just so hard!

There is so much complexity to this interaction—yet there doesn't need to be.

First, some perspective for her: her time planning with him wasn't wasted. Getting the right support systems in place takes time and multiple attempts. We encourage couples to think of it as an arc across a number of different events and experiments until the ADHD partner's mindset, skillset and plan align with what he wants to accomplish and with his partner's responses. This was just one event. It doesn't define success or failure—unless you let it.

Second, ADHD isn't fair—for either of you. In fact, dealing with it is a huge pain in the you-know-where. But to be angry about the fact that he has ADHD would be like saying it's unfair that your partner has one leg missing and accommodations need to be made because of it. With ADHD you can't "see" the struggle ahead and prepare for it by arranging your expectations around accommodations you will need to make. The bitterness of her situation comes in part from the distance between what she imagined she would get in her relationship (the perfect husband) and what she ended up with (the imperfect husband.) This is one reason why accepting the presence of ADHD and grieving for the fact that it is there can be so healing. Once you BOTH stop railing against the unfairness of it and start approaching it from a "this isn't what I expected, but it's the hand I've been dealt—so what next?" point of view, things do get easier. That distance between expectation and reality shrinks. Take what you have and make it better.

Third, about her hopes getting dashed...Learning to manage ADHD is a long process. There are very few situations in which a single conversation will be a turning point—particularly when it comes to working on one small area of the relationship. More likely, the ADHD partner in your relationship will work and experiment, and work some more. Sometimes he will fail. The non-ADHD partner will work and experiment and work some more. She too will sometimes fail. And the reliability factor in the relationship will slowly improve, as will the warmth factor. One day the two of you will take stock and realize that things have gotten better. You will sigh a sigh of relief and warily look around to make sure the ADHD demon isn't going to steal it all away again. If you are smart, you will celebrate your successes. You are on the road to recovery. You've got some victories under your belts and you are starting to get the hang of it.

But the worst thing about their bedtime argument is that it makes them adversaries. In her fury and his response to her anger, the other partner becomes the bad guy. Instead, they could be aligned as partners against the *real* problem—the ADHD symptoms.

There are other responses that would have made them partners rather than adversaries. Here are four for this particular situation that, in their simplicity and neutrality, greatly improve the chances that this couple will continue to move ahead in a positive way:

- The *moment* she starts to feel anxious that he hasn't come upstairs yet, she acts on her feelings and comes downstairs to alleviate her anxiety (rather than let it build). She asks something like, "You said you were coming upstairs. Have you changed your mind? I'm trying to figure out whether or not to turn off the lights." This is not parenting. She is not instructing him on what to do—she is simply responding to her own feelings and figuring out her own next move.
- She waits until she is ready to turn out the lights, determines he's not there and puts a flashlight outside the door. This is their agreed-upon signal not to wake her up when he comes in. At a different time (when they aren't both tired) they figure out the reason he didn't make it upstairs.
- When he starts to watch the game, he quickly runs upstairs and notifies her so she isn't left hanging and won't get anxious. (This response tends to be a hard one for those with ADHD, particularly if distraction is the reason he got into the game.)
- He sets an alarm to remind himself to get up and go upstairs at a time they agreed on. He might even enlist his child: "I've promised your mom I'll go to bed at 10 p.m. and have set an alarm for that. When it goes off, boot me out of the room!"

These all share some characteristics. They are respectful and straightforward. They assume that each person is responsible for him or herself and can exercise free will, even if it's not in everyone's best interests. They assume that the ADHD partner is genuinely interested in improving his or her reliability, and that changing behaviors is a long-term process.

Anger and the Illusion of Control

It takes non-ADHD partners a long time to come to the understanding that they have zero control over ADHD. And by the time they do, they are often burned out and angry.

> ***ADHD partner:*** *My partner says my ADHD is my problem and that I need to "fix it." Until I do she is pretty much unwilling to engage with me in any way. I find this very hurtful. Also, it would be so much easier if she would at least support my efforts! How do I get her to join me in changing our relationship?*

While we are sympathetic to how hard it has been for this non-ADHD wife, her choice to withdraw seems quite severe—almost as if she is trying to *force* her husband to change. "If it's painful enough," the thinking goes, "perhaps he'll fix it." Or maybe a therapist has told her to completely disengage. We urge you to avoid this approach. Not only is it hurtful but it's also probably inefficient. Since some of what this couple needs to "fix" is related to their interactions, she has effectively impaired his ability to improve their situation at least some of the time. She has abdicated responsibility, and it's hard to imagine that *disengaged* is the best she can offer this relationship. Instead, she should remove herself from taking on his responsibilities but remain engaged in supporting his efforts for change with a positive and open attitude.

Her anger and retreat from him may be a way of trying to manipulate change, but such a strategy often backfires. We're guessing that many ADHD partners will be able to sympathize with this man's statement:

> **ADHD partner:** *We suffer from what I call the "leeway conundrum." My wife, the non-ADHD spouse, has "leeway" if she makes a mistake. But in her hyper-organized world I, the ADHD spouse, do not. If I were "normal" I would have leeway, but no leeway for me because too much is too much, and one more mistake just adds to "too much." This puts huge pressure on me, yet I see no way around it. And if I try to just let it go or not worry, that is counter-productive to the principle goal of improving behavior. Of course, improvement requires hyper-vigilance, which triggers my fear/stress reaction and also sometimes gets me in trouble. Do other couples have this issue?*

This man has started to master his ADHD symptoms but is not always consistent. His wife is still wary and determined to keep him in line. Her "threat" is that of disapproval and anger. Yet this threat sometimes triggers a stress response that gets in his way. Worse, her double standard clearly infuriates him, and his resulting anger will pop up somewhere else. He will rebel in some way or, at a minimum, continue to harbor resentment for her parenting behavior.

Her strategy *may* work in the very near-term. This man is on his toes. But he's not happy, and he's certainly not harboring positive feelings towards his wife. Nor is she feeling warmly towards him. She must remain in a negative and vigilant mindset to continue her threatening posture—and this mindset is not conducive to a thriving relationship. Instead of *dominating* him, as she is here, she needs to respect his right to work on his issues in his own way. We admit that this is a challenge, and it brings non-ADHD partners back to the perennial question: *if I don't motivate change in our lives, will it actually happen?* We argue you must put your dreams of forcing your partner to change aside. To change behavior, you need a paradigm shift.

Paradigm Shift Releases You From Anger

(Question sent to Melissa): *You mentioned you let go of your anger cold turkey, which not many can do. How do I get to a place of acceptance that I cannot change my ADD spouse? I logically know I can't change him but emotionally I'm not accepting that.*

Everyone becomes angry once in a while. What Melissa got rid of was the anger of feeling that *her life and her husband's ADHD were awful all the time.* She did it by thinking about *herself* instead of her husband, and realizing that she simply did not *like* the angry, resentful person she had become. She vowed to no longer be that person, and let her life proceed as it would as a result.

Like the woman asking this question, she knew rationally that she wasn't in control of her husband, but that didn't help her emotionally accept this. Her life, to this point, had been one of actively pursuing what she most wanted…and often getting it. She figured, "If I just work hard enough, somehow he will change." But the reality of her lack of control was finally forced upon her. Her husband demonstrated this, in no uncertain terms, by having an affair. Happily, you can learn from her experience, sans the affair. The question to ask yourself is *what do I really, truly, control?* There is only one answer to that question: *myself.* And for ADHD partners who struggle with symptom management, even controlling yourself can feel like a stretch.

Too many partners, particularly non-ADHD partners, get sucked into what could be labeled the *illusion of control.* You get angry, your partner responds. Perhaps he leaves the room and stops the discussion. Perhaps she finally does what you ask of her. Perhaps he breaks down in tears and apologizes. You get a feeling that you have some control when you express anger and your partner responds. But that is just your partner's *superficial* response. Underneath that response is another, more important one—an unhealthy emotion that grows in direct response to the manipulation.

Your chronic anger works against the respect, love, caring, empathy, romance and anything else good that you wish to build in your relationship. When you attack or manipulate a partner, you also attack your own relationship. Put another way, your anger hurts you at least as much as it hurts your partner. Every episode of chronic anger moves you further away from your goal of having a healthy, loving relationship regardless of whether your anger creates short-term gain. Again, we aren't saying that you should never get angry. But anger that is used to manipulate another always hurts you.

This is what Melissa internalized when she stopped being angry. She realized that she did not control her husband and never would. Not only was she suffering from the illusion of control, but her anger was also turning her into someone whom she didn't want to be. The only solution for that was to start being the person she *did* want to be. And that's when she put her anger aside "cold turkey." She decided the most important thing was to be—and act like—a person she loved, and to share that person with those around her. How her husband responded was up to him.

This is a different response from announcing to your partner that "ADHD is your problem…get back to me when you fix it." By staying engaged but focusing only on being her best self, not on what George needed to fix, Melissa untangled the power and control struggle that had been going on in the relationship. By staying engaged and positive, she communicated that she was supportive, but also independent. She was no longer willing to lose herself in a relationship dominated by ADHD symptoms and responses. He could act however he was going to act…she was going to hold herself to her own high standards.

Understand that when you take anger away from what has been a chronically angry relationship, you create a vacuum. You are no longer pushing your partner to perform in a certain way and he (or she), therefore, cannot push back in response. You are doing what Harriet Lerner, in *The Dance of Anger*, calls "stepping out of the cycle of anger," and your relationship is changed *by definition*. But you don't really know how your partner *will* start responding once your pushing stops. Will he stop working on making the relationship better? (This is a HUGE fear of non-ADHD partners as they contemplate moving away from anger!) Will she lose interest? Will the ADHD take over? Will he stay with his girlfriend and send you divorce papers? You don't (and can't!) know. Please hear us when we tell you that it *doesn't matter* what the ADHD partner's immediate response is. What matters is that you have decided to become a person whom you like and that you behave consistently with that image of your best self. When you live your life as your best self, good things will follow.

And, in fact, this is what happened to Melissa. Most important about this paradigm shift was that she started to immediately feel better about herself. Her life opened up again, and she realized that she was free to make her own choices. She was lighter, happier, and more generous in her thinking towards herself and others. This did not go unnoticed. George's responses, in sequence, were:

1. **Surprise:** His chronically angry wife had disappeared.
2. **Relief:** Melissa was finally nice to be with again. Even difficult conversations were calmer and more rational.
3. **Hope:** Could it be possible that this change was permanent?
4. **Surprising feelings of love:** This is the woman I originally fell in love with! I didn't realize just how much I missed her.

George asked, rightly, "Is this real? How do I know you will stay this way?" The only truthful answer is, of course, that no one can predict the future. But Melissa was committed to this change because it was for *her*, not for him, and this is what she told him: "I know I've reoriented myself permanently, but of course the only way that you'll know that is to observe it." She simply would not let her life move again in a direction that so brought her down.

This did not mean that ADHD symptoms and disagreements suddenly disappeared. But it did mean that at least one party was no longer willing to be held hostage. Either they would carefully negotiate their way out of their mess and work constructively together, or their marriage would end.

Talking about divorce in a book that is about thriving in your relationship is probably not what you expected. But what we are really talking about is choice. As counselors, we work to help people bring their best selves to their relationship because we understand that doing so creates the best environment for falling in love again. It is your best selves that you fell in love with way back when...and those good people are still inside. You do not give your relationship an adequate chance to be happy and fulfilling *until* you yourself bring that best self forward.

The *only* change that you can create is change within *yourself*, not within your partner. So find the good person inside you and bring him or her to your relationship! But please internalize that this is the best you can do. You cannot force your partner to do the same. You offer yourself, you invite your partner...and then you see what happens. It's a leap of faith...except that it's not. Because it's a BIGGER leap of faith to think that by being *angry* you can manipulate things to make your relationship better, even though you know that the human response to anger is more anger.

Nine Anger Busters

So far we've explored common sources of anger in ADHD-impacted relationships and alluded to some of the ways that you can start to address your anger. Here we would like to spell out some specific strategies. We call them *anger busters.*

Anger Buster 1: Nurture Your Relationship

A webinar participant recently asked Melissa, "Even if we fix our relationship, are we always going to need to think about the ADHD?" Our answer is a qualified yes. Relationships only thrive when they are *nurtured.* How many times have you heard a couple say they divorced because they "grew apart?" They simply stopped thinking about their relationship and focused on other things.

Relationships impacted by ADHD require certain kinds of *active nurturing,* including:

- A constant vigilance that you are *attending* to each other, to fight distractibility and loneliness
- Ongoing negotiation to bridge your differences
- Searching for ADHD-friendly ways to support organizational challenges
- Keeping parenting behaviors at bay
- Seeking out the positive in each other

As your relationship becomes more and more positive in tone, this vigilance becomes easier and easier—but it should never go away.

Active nurturing is an ongoing effort that allows ADHD to play a much smaller and significantly more neutral role in your relationship. When ADHD is not the main event, but just another aspect of a relationship, couples can focus on the things they love about each other and thrive. But don't mistake the positive result with the idea that this comes with no effort. It takes vigilance and patience to live with ADHD, whether you are the person who has it or the partner of someone who has it. So always remember to make nurturing your relationship a very top priority in your life. Cut out other obligations to make sure you have enough time for each other, and schedule attend time regularly.

Anger Buster 2: Take Control

In her landmark book, *The Dance of Anger,* Harriet Lerner notes that anger is *inevitable* as long as you are "giving in and going along" in your relationship. This is a good description of what partners do when the impact of ADHD gets to be too much. Each, in their own ways, "gives in" or loses control of their lives to ADHD symptoms that are either undiagnosed or undermanaged. To lessen that inevitable anger, partners need to take back control the way Melissa and George did. ADHD cannot and will not be king!

> ***Non-ADHD partner:*** *I understand that you've said I can become less angry when I take control of my life…exactly how do I go about doing that and stop my unproductive responses? They have become automatic for me.*

Taking back control is a process. To start out, there are some emotional hurdles you need to overcome:

1. **Confront your hardest emotions**—Fear, anger, denial, hopelessness: these are obstacle emotions that can really get in your way. Confronting them means identifying them and then internalizing that only you are responsible for your emotions and the actions you take. You'll also want to learn about the source of your emotions and filters so you can confront and manage or change them.
2. **Acknowledge the legitimacy of your own and your partner's emotions**—This helps you gain acceptance of your situation and makes it easier to hear each other for the purpose of constructively responding to your emotions.

3. **Forgive yourselves** so you may move forward and not be stuck in your past.
4. **Seek what you love about yourself** so you can "be" that person again.

Then there are the tactical parts of the process:

- Refusing to engage in the cycle of anger or parent/child dynamics.
- Optimizing treatment for ADHD and other medical issues in the relationship.
- Developing communication techniques that communicate respect and caring.
- Negotiating your differences as equals.
- Getting ADHD support structures in place and learning how to interact with them.
- Doing whatever is necessary to make the ADHD partner reliable enough to improve trust.
- Learning to think in a positive way about where you are going.

All of these elements contribute to regaining control over yourself and your relationship. We urge you to carefully consider how you might implement them in your life.

Anger Buster 3: Take a Third-Person Look at Your Actions

It's not uncommon to experience anger, fear, denial and hopelessness. Unfortunately, we tend to justify bad behaviors based on experiencing those emotions. You might think, for example, *I screamed at my partner because he never follows through on what he says!* Instead, we suggest you take a third-person look at your own behavior. There are some *absolutes* when it comes to how we should treat any person. The fact that you are close to someone should encourage you to give that person the *best* possible treatment. Saying, "I've had a hard day and am tired. I know I can let down my guard because I'm at home now" doesn't cut it when the result is that strangers and friends get better treatment than your life partner.

After you've had an argument, we urge you to step back and ask yourself these questions: *If I saw a friend treating his or her partner the way I just treated mine, what would I think? Would I admire that behavior?* Other good questions to ask are these: *If my partner treated me the way I just treated my partner, would I feel I had been fairly treated? Would it make me feel warm all over, or at least respected?* These are particularly good questions to ask yourself if you tend to delegate, nag or boss around your partner, or if you use ADHD symptoms as an excuse for behavior that is hurtful to your partner—especially when you are not making all efforts to change your hurtful behavior.

We've offered the quotes and stories in the first part of this chapter specifically so that you can read them and say, "Uh oh, that's me!" and start to both identify and confront your own behavior. You may not yet know what to do about these difficult emotions, but we hope that you will now have the *motivation* to find out how to "fix" *yourself* rather than your partner.

Take control of your own actions. The "inevitable" anger that results from "giving in and going along" will diminish.

Anger Buster 4: Use Good Fights and Commiserate

We reviewed good fights in the communications chapter on pages 66-80. If you develop the habits necessary to fight respectfully, soothe difficult conversations and make and accept bids for repair, you significantly improve the chances that you will thrive as a couple. Anger won't go away completely, but that destructive, chronic anger will be replaced by episodic anger that signals a need to negotiate.

One very effective anger buster is to accept the legitimacy of negative emotions. Let's face it—there is a *reason* that each of you became angry...your lives have not turned out as you thought they would because ADHD symptoms (and responses to symptoms) caught you by surprise. Instead of being adversaries as a result, you have the opportunity to *commiserate* with your partner and validate his or her pain, even as you continue to have disagreements over specific details of your lives just as all couples do. Imagine your partner saying, "I agree with you. It sucks that (fill in the blank) happened," or, "Wow, it would be great to be able to have this project finished. This is hanging over both of our heads!" and you can see the power of this anger buster. From a place of commiseration, rather than confrontation, the two of you can craft a plan of attack.

Anger Buster 5: Make "Good" Apologies

Everyone knows that apologizing can help repair a hurt. But have you ever apologized by saying something like, "I'm sorry I got mad at you, but I couldn't figure out why you thought going to the store right then was a good idea!" You may think you've just apologized, but you haven't. Instead, you've just blamed your partner's actions for your anger. Here's another in a similar vein: "I shouldn't have yelled at you, though I understand why I did it. You were on my case again."

A good apology doesn't include a "but" or a "because." A good apology is a statement that shows genuine contrition from inside you, without blaming your partner for your own behavior. A good apology acknowledges you didn't meet your own high standards, and accepts full responsibility for that. It demonstrates that you understand that only you are responsible for your anger, and that you blew it.

It is often difficult to offer a good apology. As humans, we look for rationalization and justification. But that just doesn't work if you are trying to *soothe your partner* with an apology. An apology filled with anger or blame doesn't feel very soothing and won't feel like an apology at all.

> ***Non-ADHD partner:*** *My husband apologizes...a lot. The problem is, they go two ways. One: he apologizes, promises to not do "it" (whatever the "it" of the moment is) again/says he'll*

try harder…and of course nothing happens. I wait and wait, and he doesn't do anything. Chances are, he's forgotten… Or two: he gives me an angry "I said I'm sorry, what else do you want from me?" because I'm still upset that he embarrassed me and I knew he didn't mean his apology in the first place. At this point, his apologies don't really mean anything to me.

Another form of not really apologizing is offering up an apology for poor actions but then not taking action to change the situation. You can say you are sorry that you forgot to do what you promised, or that you yelled at your husband. But if you do nothing to change the potential that you will do it again, have you really internalized your responsibility for the original incident? We would argue *no*.

Things get a bit tricky when an ADHD partner apologizes for ADHD symptomatic behavior that he or she hasn't gotten under control yet. What we look for in that case is 1.) an understanding that changing the behavior is desirable, coupled with 2.) a specific plan the ADHD partner is actively implementing in order to change the behavior. It might take time to optimize the approach being taken, but the act of working on the issue *to the best of one's abilities* demonstrates an internalization of the problem and a desire to fix it.

In Nancie and Steve's dual-ADHD relationship, she tends to be the more emotional of the two. In the past she has often gotten very angry. But over the past year, Nancie has worked hard to eliminate those incidents, and they are now few and far between. During a recent minor disagreement, Steve remarked that she "can be prone to those angry outbursts." Nancie was *not* happy with his feedback about behavior she hadn't exhibited in a while. After a few days had passed, and in a much calmer moment, Nancie brought up her feelings about what had occurred inside of her when he made the remark about her anger (something she had been working hard to change). Steve apologized for "sandbagging" her by bringing up old behavior that really was not pertinent to their immediate discussion. His straightforward apology, that didn't blame her, totally changed the dynamic between them, as she could sense his genuine caring and concern for her feelings.

So, making good apologies to your partner can be a wonderful way to repair from disagreements. Just leave out the "buts" and "becauses!"

Anger Buster 6: Add Touch to Sooth Your Partner

There are times when you are angry, upset, or in tears and all you want is some sort of physical reminder that your partner is there for you. In counseling, we sometimes find ourselves asking the partner of a person who is in pain, "Would it be possible for you to hug your partner right now?" The partner who isn't crying might well give us a look that communicates, "Do I dare?" The answer, most often, is yes.

Touch can be a wonderful way to soothe a partner's distress provided it is offered as a form of empathy and love. Reaching out to hold your partner's hand or providing an empathetic embrace can calm him or her, particularly if that touch is accompanied by caring words.

There are, however, times when using touch is not a good idea. If a partner is flooded and out of control with anger (rather than crying or before the flooded stage) then touching him or her might lead to a violent response. And touching to exert control is rarely healthy.

Don't be afraid to try touch if you feel there might be an opportunity. It can add much needed warmth in trying times. If you partner doesn't like the touch, he or she will let you know.

Anger Buster 7: Create Realistic Expectations

Good communication is truly important in the battle against anger and unhappiness. One reason is that it allows you to coordinate your expectations. Happiness and unhappiness are all about the gap between expectations and reality. The larger the gap, the unhappier (and often angrier) you are. So creating realistic expectations is a really important factor in managing anger.

This has some very real implications:

- It's always better to clarify expectations than to assume.
- Don't agree to do something just because you want to please your partner. Only agree to do something if you really think you can do it. Otherwise you set up unrealistic expectations.
- Don't expect that an ADHD partner will accomplish goals or tasks as quickly as the non-ADHD partner.
- Manage your expectations for the success or failure of any distinct interaction. Think about each interaction as part of a larger arc. Failure in one interaction (getting angry, not completing a chore, etc.) does not signify failure overall.
- It will take longer than you want to work out your system of thriving together. Don't expect success immediately or you may well be disappointed.
- The ADHD partner will never become non-ADHD. Managing ADHD will always take effort.

There are a lot more of these, but you get the idea. Be careful to set realistic and humane expectations for you both.

Anger Buster 8: Think Old Relationship/New Relationship

Dwelling in the past can stand in the way of your ability to step out of the cycle of anger. By holding onto past hurts you become a victim of past events that you cannot change. The best way to free yourself from the chains of past hurts is to forgive yourself—and your partner—for your past.

Yes, couples need to understand what's happening to them, but what's *most* relevant is what's happening to them *today*, not what happened before. There is no "redo" of yesterday—thinking about your past is only helpful insomuch as you can take away a lesson and apply it to change your own behavior today and tomorrow.

Melissa and George learned this lesson from Marianne McElrath, a very wise therapist with whom they briefly had the honor of working. After a few weeks of learning about their situation and listening to their stories, she announced, "Next week I want you to pick up to three things that really bother each of you about your past together so you can talk about them. And then that's it. We aren't going to discuss your past again…so pick carefully!" A week later they had their session and identified their top hurts from the past. And then they looked forward.

Because dwelling in the past can be so negative for couples who had undiagnosed ADHD in their relationship, we like to encourage couples to create an *old relationship* that is separate from their *new relationship*. In your old relationship you had all sorts of bad interactions encouraged by the presence of ADHD symptoms (undiagnosed or otherwise). You responded naturally to a very difficult situation and did the best you could do, but you were not fully informed. What you ended up with was not what you wanted. And it usually included a lot of anger.

In your *new relationship,* you have an improved understanding of the impact of ADHD and responses to ADHD, as well as new tools. You also see that you can't change the past and, we hope, have accepted that past and forgiven each other. That doesn't mean that everything is fixed, but your forgiveness allows you to leave the baggage from the past where it belongs—in the past. Now you can focus on what's actually happening *today and tomorrow*. That's the concept: old relationship / new relationship. The actions that you assess and dissect are those that happened today (as in "the general present"), and the actions you choose are for the specific purpose of building something wonderful together today and in the future. When you forgive your past and, in essence, draw a line between "the bad old relationship" and today's improved efforts, you give yourselves your best chance at a positive future.

Forgiving Yourself

Forgiveness is a gift that can be challenging to give to yourself and others. In therapy, Nancie uses a powerful self-forgiveness technique that requires clients to identify the *judgments* they are holding against themselves. They might say, "I am awful," or, "I am mean," or whatever they have come to believe about themselves. They then are asked to forgive those judgments out loud: "I forgive myself for judging myself as awful. I forgive myself for judging myself as mean."

If you find you are having trouble forgiving either your partner or yourself, a good resource is Ned Hallowell's gem of a book, *Dare to Forgive*. In it he explains why forgiveness is a gift, and how to follow the specific steps of forgiveness.

Anger Buster 9: Set Standards for Yourself…and Act on Them

One of the most effective delineators between the old relationship and the new one is the standards you set for yourself. In various ways we have recommended setting a high bar for your own behavior—treating your partner with respect, for example, or deciding that you can't be, and don't wish to be, in charge of your partner's responsibilities or anger. We urge you to think about who you are when you are at your best and set standards for yourself that will help you get there and stay there. The exact characteristics you decide are important to you are, of course, up to you. But here are a few personal behaviors we think are worth considering:

- Strive to contribute your "best self" to the relationship.
- Respect yourself as well as your partner.
- Engage, don't disengage. Create opportunities to reach out to your partner in a loving way.

- Love generously, and create lots of attend time to show you care.
- Communicate your anger without attacking whenever possible. Be ready to offer and accept repairs.
- Value your relationship over your tasks.
- Show appreciation.
- Live with an open heart and forgive generously.

There are other ideas you will likely wish to add. Melissa, among other things, strives to live her life optimistically. This is part of who she is and is something she cares enough about to monitor and seek out in herself. Nancie knows how important it is to work on herself daily, and to be mindful always of bringing her best self to her relationship.

There is a strength that comes naturally from re-finding yourself and living by those personal standards you feel are most important to you. Taking control of yourself in this way allows you to lessen your anger—perhaps even to lose it completely. That doesn't immediately solve all of your problems. Your own or a spouse's ADHD symptoms will likely still remain in need of better management. But the environment in which the two of you will be dealing with them will be radically altered. And that can make all the difference.

Is It Finished Yet? Navigating Chores, Tasks and Life Balance

" Housework can kill you if done right."

— Erma Bombeck

Figuring out how to split the responsibilities of life is an issue in virtually all committed partnerships. Let's face it, a lot of that stuff isn't fun, there's a lot of it, and life is short! The following statistics about chore distribution for couples make a good backdrop to a chapter about chores and division of labor (Parker-Pope, 2010, p. 192-98):

- Women who don't work outside the house do an average of 38 hours a week on housework, while their husbands do about 12. When both partners work outside the house, the numbers change to about 28 hours a week of housework for women and 16 for men.
- When women get married, they add about 70% *more* time to completing household chores, while men average 12% *less* after their wedding day.
- When women are the sole breadwinners, and husbands are home, women *still* do more housework on average.

- Due to gender stereotyping reinforced in families, many men grow up without learning how to complete basic household chores such as laundry and cooking. We speculate that this trend might be more pronounced for boys with ADHD, as their parents might choose to do tasks for them rather than patiently teach all of the sequencing, planning, time management and reminder skills needed for chore management and completion.

Why are we giving you this information? We want you to know it's not all about ADHD. On the other hand, as you read on, you will see that ADHD symptoms (and interactions around those symptoms) often don't help the situation either. We hope this chapter will provide inspiration about how to balance your life responsibilities when it comes to chores, tasks and ADHD. Doing so is really relevant as you seek to thrive together. Research suggests marriages are much happier when women (sorry, guys!) feel chores are divided well enough. It doesn't have to be equal—and as the statistics above demonstrate, it probably won't be—you just need chores "well enough" distributed to satisfy her.

There is a silver lining to that news. Surveys and interviews with 300 men done by Neil Chethik, author of a book about what men are looking for in marriage, found a consistent parallel between housework and sex. He noted that "the happier wives were with the division of housework, the happier their husbands were with their sex lives." (Parker-Pope, 2010, p. 208) Women who say that "chores are foreplay" aren't kidding!

One more note. Organizing tasks better is often (though not always) a concern driven by non-ADHD partners. While we make the case that more organized partners should not be in control of chores and responsibilities, we also allow that they will likely continue to be the driving force behind encouraging progress in this area. That seems necessary if for no other reason than it is a reflection of their greater interest in the topic.

And with that, we will move on to what to do about this troubling area in many relationships!

HOTSPOT 13
Overwhelmed by Chores and Parenting

We regularly hear from non-ADHD partners like the non-ADHD husband who told Melissa, "My wife with ADHD has never fully focused on our kids, in my opinion, and I have spent a lot of time being the responsible one. Over the course of our marriage, my life became one of crushing responsibility." Melissa herself remembers well what it felt like to be responsible for practically everything that had to do with family and home care. For a while, the distribution of chores in her home felt completely imbalanced. Her husband had to *work* while she had to *work, shop, cook, raise the kids, and take all responsibility for everything else, too.* She'll admit that this description isn't completely fair. Melissa and George have the pictures to prove that they went places with their kids together, that George took the kids to the park across the street, and that they did get out together. And George reminds her that he took the 4 a.m. feeding each night when their children were newborns. But when it came to the household dreck, it was pretty clear who was the more motivated and in charge. After a while, "crushing responsibility" is exactly what it felt like.

Undiagnosed ADHD symptoms contributed greatly to this issue. It was easy for George to become distracted by—and engaged with—things more *interesting* than changing the latest dirty diaper, going to the grocery store for more milk, or calling animal control to get the raccoons out from under the porch. Disengaging from the home office computer was hard enough because of his ADHD. Trying to do so to fold and put away the laundry when his wife was also capable of doing it seemed almost impossible. He simply could not muster the motivation.

> ***Non-ADHD partner:*** *My ADHD spouse and I are facing unavoidable and persistent responsibilities right now as we are raising a baby. This has become particularly challenging for me as I find myself "parenting" him. I would like more ways to work with my ADHD spouse to have* ***him*** *remember that the daycare payment is due or to notice that my daughter needs her sheets changed, etc. How do I get my husband to initiate and partner more with childcare decisions?*

Adding kids to your lives is a *huge* stressor and contributor to the chore wars. Before children, non-ADHD partners may have compensated successfully (and without too much resentment) for ADHD disorganization. We're not saying this compensating behavior was a good thing, only that this is what probably happened. Then came kids. Children not only add financial stress to many relationships but also put the need for better organization at home on steroids. There is simply a greater volume of work that needs to be done, and lots of it is not very interesting. Plus, the work is 24/7, and safety issues become more pressing when you are responsible for children. As if all of this weren't enough, you are both getting less sleep—increasing the presence of ADHD symptoms just as you need a *greater* ability to focus.

Hidden Expectations

We're not telling you anything new here. Ask almost any couple about their lives pre-kids, and they will tell you they have no idea how they could have thought they were so busy before! But there are often a few hidden stumbling blocks when couples start families. A non-ADHD partner might expect the arrival of a child to focus a previously distracted partner. Similarly, a non-ADHD partner might expect the ADHD-partner to be able to manage the extra workload *because that's what adults do.* These expectations are often not met. The ADHD symptoms that got in the way before still remain for the ADHD partner. Furthermore, the increased pressure from schedules, lack of sleep, and a now harried non-ADHD partner can create a paralyzing feeling of being overwhelmed. Because of ADHD (and perhaps a gender-gap lack of skills), this woman's husband needs to double down on creating a reminder system that enables him to *notice* and help out. If he's overwhelmed, he may disengage instead.

Maternal Gatekeeping

Undiagnosed ADHD symptoms contributed to George's lack of effort at home. It was *genuinely* difficult for him to find the motivation to engage in something as boring as housework and to stay focused on the huge list of tasks that are part of raising a family. But it is important to acknowledge that it's not *just* ADHD or the additional stress of family. For many couples, *maternal gatekeeping* also plays a role. This is when one partner (usually the woman, but it could be a man, in which case it would be paternal gatekeeping) has strongly-held ideas of how things "should be" around their home. If her partner does it another way, at a different time, or with a slightly different outcome, a gatekeeper will correct, criticize or "educate" her partner to do it better. He cleans the windows but leaves some streaks. Sets the table but leaves out the spoons ("We never use spoons!"). Does the laundry but leaves it in the dryer to get wrinkled. A gatekeeper will voice an opinion about these things. She feels her way is right and can usually tell you why ("When you set the table it's the custom to include spoons!").

Unfortunately, maternal gatekeeping has the unintentional result of discouraging the involvement women seek from their partners. Gatekeepers send mixed messages. "I want you to be involved" is side-by-side with "you don't do things well enough. What's wrong with you?"

This came up for Nancie and Steve when it came to doing the laundry. Early on, there was one basket for laundry, and whoever was doing the laundry would need to sort through it to determine what was to go into hot water, what was to go into warm water, etc. Once when Steve was doing the laundry, something red got mixed in with the whites. Nancie was displeased with the resulting pink clothes and let Steve know it loudly and clearly. As a result, Steve no longer wanted to, in any way, be involved with doing the laundry. However, he brilliantly went out and bought a three-bag laundry cart. He's the ADHD creative thinker/engineer in the family, so this was an easy solution for him. They now have an understanding about what goes in which bag, and laundry is no longer an issue.

We urge all couples to do their best to eliminate maternal gatekeeping in their relationship. Give it a name and fight against it. Question the status quo when it comes to "who knows best." Stop nitpicking and instructing. Sometimes there *is* a best way to do something—for example, when it comes to safety. But lots of times there are simply *different* ways to do things. Recognize that there are times when a creative solution is what is called for, and do your best to come up with one together.

Take a Balanced Assessment

When one or both partners feels overwhelmed by chores and parenting, we urge you to take a balanced look at what might be going on. You might find:

- ADHD behaviors, such as difficulty planning or remembering, are getting in the way.
- Maternal/paternal gatekeeping has discouraged the less dominant partner.
- You are overcommitted.

- You are in a difficult stage in your life—one in which *no one* feels they have enough time. The classic period for this is when you have children under the age of 6.

If ADHD behaviors are causing the problem, you need to focus first on improving ADHD treatments across the first two legs. If the issue is maternal gatekeeping, then you need to stop the gatekeeping while also creating opportunities for the ADHD partner to step up and take on more responsibility. If over-commitment is the root of the problem, then the first plan of attack would be to cut some things out of your lives. And if you are in a tough stage of your life, we urge you to accept that you can't possibly do it all. Focus first and foremost on what's most important—making sure all members of your family are safe and feel well-loved.

Accept Different Approaches

You will want to tackle any power imbalances in your relationship because you will not thrive unless you do. And as you do so, you will likely be struck by just how differently you accomplish chores. One person might take off his clothes at night near the closet and then put things away. The other might throw clothes into a big pile on the floor of the closet…and find what to wear in that pile the next day. Both approaches actually work—each person knows how to find the clothes he or she needs and has a "method" of getting ready for bed.

Couples benefit greatly when they acknowledge the *legitimacy* of their different approaches. Within reason, it does not matter if you do something in a sloppy way—as long as it doesn't negatively impact your partner. So if clothes start to stink, or the piles start to migrate to the living room, then the conversation needs to turn to the *impact* of the choice that has been made. Remember, chores don't need to be balanced—they only need to be balanced well enough for couples to feel happy about household work distribution. There is room for inventiveness and different ways to get things done.

Too many non-ADHD partners secretly (or not-so-secretly) view the chore wars as a campaign to *get things done right*, rather than two different approaches that need to be *negotiated*. And too many ADHD partners view disorganization as a sort of immutable "law" of nature. For many, this is the only way they have known, and it's hard to see that it can cause genuine discomfort for others.

The only victory in this "chore war" comes when both partners negotiate as equally respected partners. Though both partners may harbor a great deal of resentment about the distribution of tasks, you really do want the same thing—to keep your lives in order *well enough* so you can get on with the fun stuff (living your dreams and loving each other!).

Get Buy-In

It's important to get an ADHD partner's (and particularly, an ADHD man's) buy-in to the idea that running a household is a job that takes more than one person and that he can do more. We've seen a lot of approaches over the years, and what doesn't work is nagging or calls for "fairness," which are too easily written off and too likely to put an ADHD partner on the defensive. Dictating what will happen is also not a great strategy for many couples because doing so tends to reinforce parent/child dynamics.

What *does* seem to work is a straightforward approach: *I've tried to do all of this for years but simply can't any more. I don't care how we get some of this load off of my shoulders, only that we do. We're no longer talking convenience—we're talking survival.*

One benefit to this approach is that when you are talking about survival, you aren't willing to take "no" for an answer. We urge overburdened partners to consistently and constructively insist family members MUST help out in some meaningful way, without dictating how they do it. This gives partners (and children!) the opportunity to grow into their new roles as better contributors. This is not pie in the sky. All ADHD partners are able to contribute meaningfully to household tasks if they put the right support structures in place and have the right attitude.

There is, of course, the question of whether or not all of the chores being requested are really necessary.

> ***ADHD partner:*** *I, the partner who HAS been diagnosed with ADHD, have taken on almost all of the household chores. I believe my husband has ADHD too, but he does not agree. He has more stressors than usual, including unemployment, and has become more hostile toward me and negative about everything, including our relationship, in the last 4-5 months. I continue to work myself to the bone, shopping for food, cooking, tidying the house, trying to do my own de-cluttering and job hunting while he sits in an easy chair "stroking" his tablet. Though I do also have OCD, he argues that much of what I do is not necessary so he won't help. But still, there are other things he agreed to do that he hasn't followed through on. We both feel wronged by the other…*

This woman's husband is disinterested in her household priorities. Certainly, he doesn't need to agree with her priorities and do everything his wife asks, but his lack of follow-through on the tasks he *has* promised shows things are not as they should be. Perhaps he has ADHD, perhaps he is clinically depressed, perhaps he is overwhelmed, perhaps he has an electronics addiction that is getting in the way. Or, it's possible that not doing chores is his way of asserting power in the relationship. We think this woman would benefit from putting her hurt feelings aside for a while and staying as business-like as possible as she negotiates obtaining greater participation from him. Part of their conversation should address how many of the chores she is requesting are genuinely necessary and how many of them are related to her OCD.

> ***Non-ADHD partner:*** *What do I do if my partner doesn't want to take on a task that's really important to the family?*

In the case of a specific task, rather than a pattern of behavior like the previous couple, there's a short answer to this question: find another way to get it done. Every person has the right to say no. This woman has lobbied her partner to engage and he has refused. If it's important, she'll have to get it done a different way.

Changing Chore Patterns the Businesslike Way

The businesslike approach to taming a long list of chores can work for couples with or without kids. It has five steps:

1. State the situation: *I cannot do it myself, so everyone is going to have to help out.*
2. Create a list of regular and one-time chores, and select those that are most important.
3. Determine the best fit of activity for each helper.
4. Get routines in place, including a regular meeting to coordinate your efforts efficiently.
5. Measure the success of efforts and adjust.

Have a meeting to talk about chores in an unemotional way. The household is a joint undertaking, and everyone needs to contribute in a way that reflects his or her age, capabilities and time available for work. If you disagree about how much people are actually contributing, take a baseline by tracking each person's efforts for one week and writing them down on paper or on your cell phones.

Ask for input about what each person wants to do and which chores each person in the family thinks are most important. By involving each person in assessing and picking chores, you have the highest chance of creating a good fit with schedule and inclination. For example, it probably doesn't make sense to ask someone who needs to leave the house at 7a.m. to take on a chore that takes 30 minutes first thing in the day, such as walking the dog.

You might also look for opportunities to make drudgery fun. When Melissa's kids were teens, she did laundry all in one day and dumped the clean clothes on the bed. Then, the whole family made a "date" to put on great music, fold together, and talk that evening. The kids weren't thrilled, but they didn't despise the task, either.

Yes, a non-ADHD or more organized partner will probably manage this type of business-like coordination. We think that's okay. It builds on a non-ADHD strength (organizational ability) and leads to a great outcome—chores will get better distributed and everyone's voice will get heard. *Someone* has to lead the charge.

Tips for Happily Redistributing Chores

Tip 1: **Keep your priorities straight.** Relationships are more important than stuff. Always be respectful of each other in conversations about chores.

Tip 2: **Don't cover for incomplete work.** It may be easier to "just do it," but that's the wrong type of reinforcement! Pick some other response that reinforces the importance of taking responsibility without becoming overbearing.

Tip 3: **Be compassionate about the ADHD symptom struggle.** The ability to be fully responsible for chores that weren't previously yours takes time to get right—particularly if new support structures need to be put in place.

Tip 4: **Don't become the enforcer—be an encourager and cheerleader instead.** If you have kids, make sure they are also responsible for measuring their own success (and that of others in the family).

Tip 5: **Offer training or advice if appropriate, but don't impose it.** Let others figure out what works for them. It might well be a very different system than your own. You might care about the wrinkles that result from your teen's stuffing his clean clothes in his drawer instead of folding, but he's the only one who has to wear them.

Tip 6: **Break up chores into smaller chunks** that make them seem less overwhelming and easier to tackle. This will also give you many more small victories and completions to celebrate.

Tip 7: **Start slowly and add.** Make sure one chore (or a few) are managed and fully the responsibility of the person doing the chore before adding more. This both reinforces independence and prevents feelings of being overwhelmed.

Tip 8: **Don't dictate specific times chores will get done**—this would be gatekeeping behavior. Since using a deadline as motivation is a common ADHD coping strategy, you may find ADHD family members wait until the last minute. As long as they get it done without imposing on others, that's okay.

Tip 9: **Expect tests.** Since it's easier if the more organized partner "just does it," expect others to see if you're willing to fall back into that pattern. Resist that temptation. Instead, reconvene the "family court" (if you will) and talk through the issues in a business-like way. What got in the way of the chore getting done? Would there be a better time of day? Is there a skill missing? Are you overscheduled? Is this a long-term issue or a one-time issue? Do you have the wrong chore for some reason? Pretty soon, "I didn't feel like it" will sound pretty lame to everyone, not just to you.

Tip 10: **Transition, don't abdicate**. It takes time to set up the structures necessary to succeed. If you're an organized partner, don't just hand something complex over and walk away. Be mindful of the connection between external support structures and chore reliability.

HOTSPOT 14
Tasks Don't Get Done as Promised

Once you have a chores routine in place, you may still find that an ADHD partner doesn't do those things to which he or she has committed. This can be particularly frustrating when a non-ADHD partner notices that some things get done immediately.

> **Non-ADHD partner:** *Why is it that my partner seems to be able to focus so easily on the project she is working on but just can't complete a simple household project that I've been asking about for weeks?*

Remember that ADHD is about attention dysregulation, not attention deficit. Also, unfinished chores are *not* a sign that your partner doesn't love you. They are a sign that 1.) ADHD is getting in the way and your partner doesn't have the structures in place to get the job done or 2.) your partner doesn't actually want to do the chore. Don't take it personally—remain calm, and discuss what the issues might be, including these ADHD-related ones:

- ***Project planning issues:*** Executive function issues may make it difficult to plan and sort out steps. This not only complicates the process of planning but can also lead to embarrassment about struggles with things "others do so easily."
- ***Overscheduling:*** Difficulty comprehending time, and remembering past experiences with time, can lead to optimistically taking on far more than is really possible.
- ***Distraction:*** While doing a task, the partner gets distracted from it—making the task take too long (if he or she even comes back to it!).

- ***Boring tasks are harder to focus on:*** Those with ADHD do better focusing on things of interest than things that bore them.
- ***Immediate things capture attention easily:*** An unfortunate side effect of having ADHD is that *immediate* things often capture the attention more rigorously than *important* things. This means even important tasks can get put aside for whatever interesting thing is going on in the moment.

What can be even more frustrating is when a partner breaks a previous promise and chooses to do something a non-ADHD partner feels is frivolous, such as wasting time on a computer or watching TV.

> **Non-ADHD partner:** *I agree that every person has the right to change his or her mind, but is it always okay, even when the change is hurtful, disrespectful and selfish? For example, my husband and I planned, discussed and amicably agreed to paint the ceiling and walls of our rental property. His job was the ceiling while I agreed to paint the walls after he was done. We both decided he could play golf after his task was complete. However, by golf time he had only painted half of the ceiling. At first I was calm and reminded him of his commitment to the task. Paint first, golf later. But he became defiant and insisted he had made a commitment to his golf partners. I reminded him that his commitment to his wife of 33 years was more important. He became very angry and reminded me that only the week before I had left him to the task of painting to attend something for myself. My commitment was planned 6 months earlier, and, try as I might, I couldn't get out of it. A horrendous screaming match followed, with me in tears begging him to stay and finish before he left for his game. He left! From that moment on my feelings for him changed and I struggle to stay in this marriage. That was the last straw.*

Flexible Thinking

In spite of her husband's lack of empathy for her position, this woman could have recovered from her husband's poorly timed decision. In this case, the choice to play golf wasn't in the best interests of the relationship, but it is still his choice to make. At that point, his wife is faced with a question: *What now?* She still had her task (painting the walls) to do and we hope she proceeded without him.

Thinking flexibly when faced with a change in plans is a skill we urge all non-ADHD and other-ADHD partners to develop. You'll benefit greatly if the unexpected speed bumps in your relationship don't turn into mountains. You can't force your partner to paint the ceiling right now, and we don't recommend taking on your partner's obligations and doing it yourself. But is there another approach you could take that would move you forward?

With more flexible thinking, their conversation could have gone something like this:

Him: *I'm going to play golf.*

Her: *But you promised to finish the ceiling first!*

Him: *Yes, but I made a promise to my golf buddies, too.*

Her: *That's really disappointing to me. I was so looking forward to getting this done today. We need to get it done so we can rent the apartment out. Okay, give me a moment to think about how to respond to this…You'll be finishing your game in about five hours. Can you come back and finish the ceiling then?*

Him: *Yes, I suppose so.*

Her: *Okay. It's not perfect, but I'm going to finish the walls while you are gone. So if you drip paint on the walls, you'll need to touch them up. I'll leave you the paint if I'm not still here.*

She still may have experienced some hurt feelings because he chose golf over something she deemed important. But she could talk with him about this later, within the context of their larger relationship and any other times he has similarly put her second. Requests to fix *patterns of behavior* seem easier to consider than an individual event. If she had taken this approach would she now be thinking about divorce? Sadly, we'll never know.

The Desire to Please

While discussing the golf game vs. painting dilemma in the seminar in which it arose, a different man with ADHD noted that sometimes promises are made that, by their nature, cannot be kept. For example, he understands how in debt he is to his wife for all that she has put up with in their relationship. When she asks for something, his first response is to say "yes." He does this even before he considers whether he's free or whether he has the time or the skills. He simply wants to do as much as he can for her, and this wish overrides his good sense. Luckily, his wife has caught on. Now when she asks him if he can commit to something, she makes sure they discuss the details of that commitment. This acts as "brakes" for him, and they are more likely to come to a realistic resolution. He then goes on to do his best to please her…but with more realistic expectations on both sides. The more realistic expectations mean that he is more likely to be successful.

Feeling Overwhelmed

Another reason ADHD partners don't take on tasks has to do with feeling overwhelmed.

> ***Non-ADHD partner:*** *I am trying not to parent or nag to get chores and important tasks done. For example, the taxes are three years overdue and my spouse's driver's license expired two years ago and needs out of state papers and a doctor's note to be renewed. So far my ADHD spouse doesn't want to participate…or perhaps can't?*

We commonly run into clients with multiple years of back taxes. Taxes might be the least interesting and engaging thing in the entire world—no wonder it's hard to follow up on them when you have ADHD! The project just seems too big and too complex to wrap your arms around. Feelings of being overwhelmed take over. A great way to manage this feeling is "chunking."

Chunking

The best way to attack overwhelming projects is in small pieces. For a deadline-specific project such as taxes, you might give each chunk of the project its own schedule:

Monday, 7:30–8:00 p.m.—locate receipt boxes in basement, move to office

Tuesday, 8:00–10:00 p.m.—sort receipts in box A

Thursday, 8:00–10:00 p.m.—sort receipts in box B

Saturday 10:00 a.m.–1:00 p.m.—look up all deductible donations

Further, you want to make each decision in the process as easy as possible. To make each individual sorting decision easier, for example, you might label your piles or use labeled boxes. *Does this receipt go in this pile or that one?* If the piles are labeled, the answer will come more easily.

With this sort of *chunking* you a.) know you can make your deadline if you stay on track, b.) have a better view of how long it will take and c.) have an early warning system if either partner isn't on schedule. And here's a tip: if you can create a system that involves working together (for example, sorting receipts together while listening to the radio) you will be more likely to make your deadline. Having a "buddy" helps keep distracted adults on task.

A weekly meeting to make sure you are both in agreement about the priorities for that week will also help. If you feel strongly that getting the license renewed is a very top priority, but your husband feels ordering computer equipment is more important, you need to negotiate so you are both informed and can make a decision together about who does what, and when, without hard feelings.

If a partner doesn't seem to want to participate, ask him if he doesn't want to or "can't." He'll know. His answer will help you decide on your next steps. Even if he refuses to budge, at least you'll know what you're dealing with.

HOT SPOT 15
Differences in Tolerance for Chaos

> **Non-ADHD partner:** *My husband makes piles and messes everywhere and doesn't even notice them. As the years have passed, I've ultimately given up and given in—I don't want to cause a fight. But the mess causes a great deal of frustration for me and makes me physically uncomfortable at home. I think that we eventually will try to confine the piles and messes to one area where he can spread out, but how do we get caught up? Thinking about cleaning and organizing is incredibly overwhelming to my husband, and I find it upsetting to think about tackling this myself. Help!*

This woman's husband is not aware of the chaos around him. This is not unusual, though it is not characteristic of everyone with ADHD. (Some with ADHD become quite careful about creating order, as it is how they manage to hold their lives together.) Those who are tolerant of the mess often make their partners quite uncomfortable. Some non-ADHD and other-ADHD partners admit they actually dread walking through the door. Others become quite anxious about chaos in their lives in general and worry that the inconsistency of their ADHD partner means they must always be on alert. The physical mess is just one manifestation of a larger problem.

To thrive, you must negotiate a solution to any differences in tolerance for chaos you may have. Do not, if you have ADHD, assume that just because you've always lived in chaos it is okay to make your partner physically ill with anxiety or stress over your mess. Likewise, if you are a non-ADHD partner, don't assume that keeping a home very neat will be comfortable for your ADHD partner. Keeping a home organized takes a great amount of effort. You may prefer to have your partner expend his or her energy on something else—such as paying attention to you.

Creating Physical and Mental Boundaries

One tactic for managing physical chaos is to create separate spaces for which each partner is responsible. This separates responsibilities, typically provides adequate visual neatness, and allows non-ADHD partners to walk away from ADHD mess while not imposing "throw this out" rules on ADHD partners. The wife above could use this tactic. Right now she is thinking about how upsetting and overwhelming it will be to tackle their backlog. This is in part because of the volume of material, but also because *she imagines significant conflict will ensue if she embarks on sorting with her husband.* So, in another version of chunking, she can separate their belongings and only "tackle" her own belongings.

To do this, locate spaces that are solely for the use of the "messy" partner (such as a basement, garage, closet, office or bedroom) and do a very broad sort. If you need assistance, hire help. Don't ask your partner. In two to four hours of undivided attention, you should be able to sort a pretty big backlog into a simple "mine" and "his." With the help of the person you hire, put the "his" stuff—*unsorted and pretty much in the order you found it—*

into the new location in a reasonably neat fashion (perhaps on shelves or in boxes marked with the date). Then, close the door if there is one. After that, the non-ADHD partner only has his own things to put away. That's both easier and more rewarding. Further, there are no arguments about what to toss out.

Once the first sort is completed, the ADHD partner can hire a professional organizer—preferably one who knows about ADHD—if he or she wants to get more organized. If he is comfortable with the disorganization, which is often the case, he can leave it as is until such time as it becomes obvious that it's in his best interests to take care of it. Non-ADHD partners should be prepared for the fact that this may be many years in the future, so it's best, once it's all sorted, to let that mess go psychologically. It's no longer your business.

To eliminate future messes from randomly accumulating, have special *his* and *hers* areas around your house. For example, in the entry or family room you might have a shelf with large baskets on it. Each partner has his or her own basket. If the mess piles up somewhere, the person who is mess intolerant can place the stuff in the appropriate basket. This doesn't take long, and it clears the space. If your partner's basket overfills, take it to his or her personal space and dump it off. This is a whole lot more efficient than arguing about whether or not the space is cleaned properly. And any time something is missing, that partner knows exactly where to look.

Sometimes, those with ADHD literally can't seem to "see" the mess around them. This can be a source of almost constant amazement for non-ADHD partners. After George started doing the dishes, Melissa noticed that everything got taken care of *except* the sink and counters, which never seemed to get washed up. While he didn't disagree that clean counters are desirable, he simply didn't seem to internalize the idea that cleaning them was part of doing dishes. George's comment was "I don't even notice the counters." Faced with a choice of really pushing the point or focusing on something more important, such as whether or not he was paying enough attention to her, Melissa simply changed tacks. Now George does all the dishes and unloads the dishwasher. Melissa cleans the counters and sinks. This new system suits both of them fine…and they get the benefit of doing it together as partners.

This compromise brings up an important point: some things are just much more important than others. Melissa will never stop insisting that George make the effort to *attend* to her. The counters? Not nearly so important. George's inability to focus on the counters wasn't personal, and it wasn't about whether or not he loved her.

The bottom line is this: if you are physically uncomfortable being in your environment or have a chore that simply isn't getting done, your resentment will build. Why not take care of it by approaching chores in a new way? Creating physical and / or mental boundaries can help.

HOTSPOT 16
My Partner Thinks He/She Knows Best

One of Melissa's all-time favorite posts at her website forum was written by a man who was enraged that his wife with ADHD did not fold her laundry and put it in the closet like "normal" people. Instead, she left it in the dryer and often walked down the hall to find clean clothes. He was looking for reinforcement for his opinion that this was outrageous behavior.

He didn't get it. Though his wife's strategy for storing clothes was not his own, it was nonetheless an excellent strategy. She was able to find her clean clothes and get to work on time.

> **Non-ADHD partner:** *How do you deal with certain ADHD coping strategies? My wife "leans" on others—including our family and, of course, me—quite a bit to do chores. This creates a lot of resentment. Also, my wife is a very social person. It's something I love and appreciate, but she often goes overboard, and I suspect she gets distracted continually during the day by friends calling, texting, etc. Any tips on how to deal with the distraction of being so social?*

Here's what's not being said in this question: *...and because she is distracted by her friends, she's not getting as much done as I think she should.* There are a whole lot of things going on here! First, the wife actually does have some effective coping strategies in place. The work is getting done because she is delegating it. This can be a great way to function if you have ADHD and have trouble getting things done...provided the delegation is to willing (or paid) help. But second, the husband doesn't like that delegation. Third, he's making a judgment call about what her priorities should be. He believes chores should come before friends.

Depending upon how much work she actually is accomplishing, it sounds as if he might be imposing his priorities on her, just as the man in the clothes folding story. And what is somewhat confusing about this is why all the others upon whom his wife is "leaning" are going along with her delegation if it doesn't make sense. It's possible that they are all enabling her to remain distracted and ineffective. If so, they aren't doing her any favors. But it's also possible that the delegation is actually a really good coping strategy—it just happens that the husband doesn't like it.

This family would benefit from getting all of their opinions out on the table, and by measuring what is actually going on. What are their mutual expectations about who needs to do what? Do they make sense? As an example, this man might assume that his wife should cook because she is at home all day. But what if she hates cooking? What if she feels strongly that the kitchen is akin to a slave galley and wants nothing to do with it? It's possible that another task would be better for her. And while they are measuring what's going on, how many hours is each of them actually spending on the household tasks, and what is each accomplishing in that time? Measuring how much each partner is doing is not that hard. Sit down together at the end of each day and make a list that carefully tracks both time spent and accomplishments for about two weeks. You'll get a good feel for what is going on. You may find that very little is getting done, even though lots of time is passing. Or, you may find that quite a lot is getting done—it's just not on the radar screen of the adult who isn't home. Once you have a real picture, you can then figure out your next steps.

Finally, talk about your mutual priorities. We personally value relationships above stuff and tasks, as long as enough gets done so your lives don't fall apart. So we're inclined to like socializing, particularly if it relates to the primary family. However, there is a point at which too much is too much. Each couple can define where that is, depending upon their situation.

Turning Around Gender Stereotypes and Chores

We're women, so we admittedly have a bias as we think about gender stereotyping. It's not explicitly stated, but we suspect that some of what is going on with the next couple has to do with this man's desire to have his wife do what she "should be" doing. In any event, hearing a non-ADHD partner try to push his or her agenda on an ADHD partner always rankles us. We ask *non-ADHD* partners, particularly women, to put themselves in the shoes of this ADHD woman:

> ***ADHD woman:*** *My husband has spent many years belittling and verbally abusing me and demanding that I do household things that I neither like nor do well. His attitude is obnoxious. What do I do?*

How do you respond to her words? Are you indignant at his obnoxious insistence? Now, turn the tables around and look at your own relationship. Are you berating and demanding that your ADHD husband do chores that he neither likes nor does well?

We are *NOT* suggesting that ADHD partners shouldn't be required to learn to do chores to support the well-being of the household. We're trying to make a point about what it feels like to have someone aggressively pursue you on the topic by asking you to take the conversation outside of typical, gender-reinforced roles.

Negotiations are in order, not dictates. And it might make sense for this couple (with the help of a counselor) to talk about what it would feel like to be the other partner. This sort of measured, respectful approach could lead this couple towards a much happier co-existence. But first he has to understand that her doing specific chores *isn't* a given…and she has to realize that contributing *enough,* in some meaningful way, *is.*

As for the verbal abuse, that's just not okay! We suggest she start to push back, hard. It's time to tell her partner—in fact ANY partner who is being verbally abusive—male, female, ADHD or non-ADHD, that this behavior is neither acceptable nor effective. Remain respectful and use the calming techniques in the communications chapter to get this message across. You can respond to verbal abuse with a statement such as "I'm not willing to respond to you when you are verbally abusive to me like that but would be happy to talk with you when you are calmer." If the abuse continues or escalates, get the help of a professional marriage counselor.

HOT SPOT 17
Work/Life Balance

Balancing work and home life is a common challenge for all adults these days. The organizational, distraction and time management issues for adults with ADHD may make finding a satisfying balance all the more challenging for couples.

> **Non-ADHD partner:** *Is it unrealistic to expect a spouse to contribute to household chores even when I am the one who stays home full time and he is the financial provider? It became immediately clear after the honeymoon that my husband does not like to do housework, and that therefore it was solely my responsibility. I understand that housework is not very stimulating or rewarding, but I can't seem to get him to understand how sometimes life just calls us to step up and help when needed. When I express the need, he just calls on one of our kids to help. Question: Should I really care who does these chores, and should I give up on the correlation between feeling prioritized/loved by his personal involvement?*

Spouses don't usually contribute in the same exact ways, but this husband's lack of contributing to household priorities has become symbolic for his wife. His lack of interest in participating at home communicates to her (whether it's true or not) that he's unwilling to meet his obligations to his family and, we suspect, that she herself is not a priority. This could happen with any couple suffering from work/life balance issues or from a disagreement about roles in the family. A husband with ADHD is probably also distracted from his wife in other ways too *because* of his ADHD symptoms. The issue of chores is simply one more indication that he's not paying enough attention.

They need to change this together. It would be healthy for this woman to not take his symptomatic behaviors personally. Nonetheless, they need to solve the larger problem. He needs to attend well enough that she knows he cares about her.

Her problem may be how she's approaching it. By asking him to "step up" because he's obligated to, she's ignoring the other obligations he is already fulfilling with his work. She also diminishes the importance of his involvement to her. (It's just another obligation.) Rather, she needs to communicate how much she appreciates his financial contributions…and also that his completion of work at home is an emotional issue for her, directly linked to how he communicates his love.

This might also be a gender or social issue—he might feel that since he's the breadwinner he's done his share. If so, he's missing an opportunity to validate her feelings by at least acknowledging her hard work and respectfully disagreeing with her instead of just brushing her off. And, if she states that this is one of the most important issues in her life, he could reconsider—not because it's interesting or fun, but because taking this action, in spite of how hard it is, will communicate *I love you*. Since this is a symbolic issue, it probably wouldn't take a huge commitment of time to turn her opinion of his interest around.

To move her concerns forward, she can approach this issue first by taking an unemotional look at his involvement with the family, outside of his financial contribution. Does he read to the kids? Coach soccer? Help with homework? Do the taxes or other financial management? Take care of odd jobs? Research cars? Run the family website?

Once there is a clear, unemotional view of his total contribution, she'll know how to move forward. They may resolve the issue with his taking on one or more chores, by adding attend time, or in some other way.

There is a larger family issue to consider, as well. This family is modeling very strict gender roles for their children. They may decide that for that reason alone it is important that he be more ready to help out. Sometimes this means cordoning off a specific household task that belongs solely to the breadwinning husband. That might be something regular such as doing laundry or dishes (easy for kids to see) or perhaps alternating cooking.

Working Too Hard

For some, the issue of balancing work and life has to do with working too many hours. Many men and women with ADHD tell us that they feel they must work very long hours because they do not work as quickly as their peers. It may take them longer to organize, plan or write. Or they may be easily distracted, leading to workplace (and home) inefficiency. In order to stay competitive, they must spend more time at work.

Some work long hours because they love the stimulation of work. Work is the most exciting thing they do, and they want more of it. Others work because they have difficulty saying *no* when a boss sends more work than they can handle in their direction. They struggle to manage it all, perhaps feeling overwhelmed. Fear of failure and low self-esteem may also play a role in whether or not some adults with ADHD are willing to set reasonable boundaries on how much work they will take on.

All of this can be really hard on the relationship. The long work hours keep you apart, thus lessening your connection. The exhaustion induced by the long hours increases ADHD symptomatic behaviors, making interactions tenser. Sex life is also often impaired. Couples are most often together at night, after calming ADHD medications have worn off. These are the hours when family demands are often the most intense.

Balancing Work and Life

Responding to work/life balance issues may be difficult, but doing so is necessary if you are to thrive. Our suggestions include:

- **Compassion:** Try to remain compassionate about the genuine struggles that face ADHD partners. ADHD really can make it difficult to stay organized and efficient at work. Your partner's dedication to staying employed is to be commended.
- **Attending:** Seek ways to increase attend time to compensate for long hours. That time might come by creating a short daily cuddle time routine, or it might come in chunks—vacations or weekends away between stints of long work hours. Pick whatever makes you each feel well enough attended.
- **Treatment:** Optimize medicinal treatment for the ADHD partner. Ask your doctor about the possibility of using a 24-hour coverage ADHD medication. If it works for you, it will improve the time that you are together in the evenings.
- **Coaching:** Consider hiring an ADHD coach who specializes in work issues. Coaches can help ADHD partners develop better support structures at work for organization, initiation and completion issues, and more.
- **Sleep and exercise:** Create a sleep and exercise routine that works for you both. When work takes up too much time, these basic treatments are likely to be more important to the overall functioning of the family and your relationship than doing chores.
- **Celebrate:** When you are together, focus on celebrating the positive. Your time is limited. Don't just focus on the problems. Make strengthening your bonds your top priority, instead.

Balancing work and life may need even larger adjustments. Take a measured look at whether or not you are asking too much of yourselves. Our lives are "crazy busy." Are your expectations realistic? Ned Hallowell's book *CrazyBusy* can help you take a look at what you might be able to cut out so that you can live your lives in line with your most important priorities. In some instances it may be a good idea to consider a dramatic change in lifestyle, such as downsizing or taking a job with a more flexible schedule…or both.

Getting Out of Your Chores and Life Balance Battles

Let's face it, lots of couples get locked into battle over how to share responsibilities in their lives, including chores, and have trouble getting out. They get stuck in their positions—convincing themselves *I'm the household slave* or, perhaps, *my partner will never appreciate either my contribution or my struggles.* We've been there ourselves, and know how hard this battle can be on both of you. Disagreements over workload are meaningful not only because all that work is hard but also because doing work with or for a partner is one way of showing you care. And lack of doing work is easily interpreted as *I don't care,* even if that isn't the case.

But the reality is that within the larger context, at least part of the chore wars may be a battle of *choice.* We decide to live our lives a certain way, and some of the tasks that life presents us are a direct result of those choices. Having children is an obvious example. When you have children, you increase your workload significantly. Always. For most, the benefit and satisfaction of having a family makes that choice almost automatic, even with the extra work. But there are a lot of other choices we make that are not so clearly beneficial…perhaps these include moving to a larger home, taking on another volunteer position in the community, or deciding to add singing lessons to an already busy schedule.

Your time is finite—both across your life span and on any given day. There is a very real limit to how much any person, or couple, can handle. We urge you to be ruthless about thinking about your priorities, and then address the chore wars (as well as the amount of attend time you spend together) by asking what's *really* important. And we urge you to not assume that one person's priorities and choices must, by default, be the choices that the other partner would make. Relentless chores, by their nature, create a black cloud that hangs over couples. To thrive, it's important to think about how to make that cloud smaller and less omnipresent. And it's important to continually remind yourselves that your relationship is priority #1.

We've given a number of different ideas for getting out of the chore wars but find that couples always want more. So we're going to give you a few overview ideas and some more examples of how they might play out in creative work-arounds in your household:

- **Eliminate**—Chances are very, very good that not everything on your list is actually critical to your survival...or to your happiness.
  - A couple sits down to analyze their to-do list with a specific goal. After writing down the list, they cross off 30% of the items by eliminating tasks they probably will never get to anyway. They also cross off lower priority items. They immediately feel better and find that the exercise helped them hone in on what they both thought was truly important.
- **Delegate**—to other people, or hired help.
  - Instead of shoveling the drive by herself (her ADHD husband had less than zero interest in this task) a wife finally hires someone to plow it.

- **Make it more fun or interesting**—Some chores can be improved through creativity and imagination.
  - It's leaf raking time again. The whole family sets aside an hour, turns on some upbeat music, and has a race to see who can build the biggest leaf pile. Afterwards they share hot chocolate.
- **Coordinate**—You can gain efficiency if you are better coordinated.
  - A family sits down twice a month and picks one "out of the norm" chore for each person to do before their next meeting. They also discuss the steps for getting that chore done. They quickly diminish the size of their to-do list while repeatedly testing for top priorities.
- **Take responsibility for your own special needs**—Don't assume your partner ought to do things that only pertain to you. This lessens resentment about chores.
  - A husband likes his work shirts to be laundered a certain way, but his wife doesn't have the time to do it for him. He does special loads with his work shirts while she does the rest of the laundry.
- **Reorient your priorities**—Put relationships with people ahead of getting things done, and you may find that the stuff becomes less oppressive while your life becomes more fun.
  - A family decides to hire a house cleaner (i.e., delegate) every other week. In between, the house can get messy. They've agreed to not complain. They know the house will get a deep clean fairly soon, and their relationship is more important than the stacks of papers. This is a big shift in their interactions.

- **Look at the bigger picture**. Though a partner may not be doing household cleaning, she may still be making a huge contribution elsewhere.
  - A husband spends time each day helping with his wife's website, for which she's eternally grateful. So she tries to do helpful things for him and remind herself that it's not just about *housework*.

Who's In Charge of What? Rebalancing Your Relationship

"You can change only what people know, not what they do."

— Scott Adams

Many unhappy ADHD-impacted relationships are defined, in part, by great inequality between the partners. This uneven power structure is one important reason the relationship is in such trouble. The more organized partner may be in charge and playing a parental role: educating, setting the rules, being the enforcer, doling out the tasks. The less organized is in a child-like role: receiving orders, seeking approval, rebelling or retreating when the pressure gets too much. These parent/child dynamics literally kill your relationship. They result in frustration and anger, are belittling to both partners, and are wildly unromantic. Simply stated, you *must* stop the parent/child pattern and balance the power between you again...even though doing so will probably feel foreign and difficult to you.

This pattern may also be described as codependent. While codependency is many things, Melody Beattie defines it this way in her classic book, *Codependent No More:*

A codependent person is one who has let another person's behavior affect him or her, and who is obsessed with controlling that person's behavior.

She also notes that "If concern has turned to obsession; if compassion has turned to caretaking; if you are taking care of other people and not taking care of yourself—you may be in trouble with codependency" (Beattie, 1992, pp. 36, 53). Codependency needs attention and treatment just as much as ADHD does. We will view power imbalances with Beattie's definition and ideas in mind.

HOTSPOT 18
Parent/Child Dynamics

Parent/child dynamics often begin with the chore wars, reviewed in the previous chapter, and often start well before couples know about ADHD. As ADHD symptoms—known or unknown—encourage inconsistency in the ADHD partner, an increasingly harried non-ADHD partner adjusts and takes on more and more responsibility. This turns out to be a mistake. Gottman's research shows a strong link between healthy relationships and those in which women, in particular, *don't* adapt to problems early in the relationship. Instead, presumably, they bring them to light right away and negotiate solutions with their partners before the problems become unmanageable.

Nonetheless, the tendency for non-ADHD or more organized ADHD partners is to compensate for the inconsistency of the ADHD partner as best they can. Non-ADHD partners have good organizational skills and often don't mind using those skills in the service of their relationship. At some point, though—often when couples start having a family, which adds significantly more complication to their lives—the non-ADHD partner cannot take on more. In order to keep her life from blowing apart at any moment, she starts to ask insistently for help. When help is not forthcoming, she takes more control. This often means becoming less forgiving of her partner's mistakes, insisting on his participation, getting angry when he can't/doesn't follow through, and pushing hard in an effort to get him to do his fair share of the work.

Of course, if the ADHD partner has undiagnosed or undermanaged ADHD, responding is a real challenge due to distractibility, poor memory, poor planning and more. In many cases, he (or she) can do the required things sometimes, but the ADHD makes him inconsistent. This is all the more frustrating for the non-ADHD partner because she sees that her partner is capable. So the ADHD partner's overall lack of focus is misinterpreted as *unwillingness* to join in or *not caring enough* about the family to do so. He is deemed a "bad" partner...and it's all downhill from there. Until this cycle is interrupted with an ADHD diagnosis and with optimal treatment, it's hard to get out of these reinforcing, negative interactions.

And unfortunately, because of the previous adaptation, the real crisis starts to hit when the non-ADHD partner is maxed out: stress is already becoming unbearable; tempers and time are short, while need is perceived more urgently. This does not make for good negotiation.

We need to point out that even though the parent figure is exerting more power in the relationship, it does not necessarily feel that way. In fact, the non-ADHD partner may act in controlling ways precisely because he or she feels completely powerless in the face of the ADHD symptomatic behaviors. This is typical of codependent behaviors. What may help couples work through this conundrum is, again, thinking about the symptoms as separate from the partner with ADHD. That way the two of you can fight as partners against the real issue—unmanaged ADHD—using the three legs of treatment.

In retrospect, it's easy to see how your relationship may have developed a codependent pattern. But that's the past. The important question is what to do now to move away from parent/child dynamics and how to remain equal, loving partners in the future.

Identifying Parent/Child Dynamics

Though it's easy to recognize when parent/child dynamics are impacting the overall relationship, it's often much harder for couples to identify individual instances of parenting or child-like behaviors.

> ***Non-ADHD partner:*** *How do I have my husband raise issues with a new therapist? For years he had a therapist who always thought everything was fine because that's what he told her. I don't want to act like a parent and "tell on him" to his therapist, but I need the therapist to know that some of his issues are very real and must be dealt with. He has debilitating anxiety, is chronically late, and can explode over something as simple as a donut.*

> ***Non-ADHD partner:*** *My husband doesn't like to be bossed around, redirected, checked up on, and the like. He makes that VERY clear. Yet he also gets mad when I don't leave him a list, wake him up when his forgets to set his alarm, or remind him of things. He can't have it both ways, and I feel damned if I do and damned if I don't. I hope you can help folks sort this sort of thing out.*

> ***Non-ADHD wife:*** *My husband agreed to take charge of carpooling to ballet class for October. I warned my husband months ago that he would have to set things up ahead of time because that's a busy time for him. I even gave him ideas about how to do it. It's now October and last week he came to me to ask if I would be his backup for carpooling because he's*

so busy this month. When he also started asking questions about the logistics of carpooling, I lost it! I was so angry that he didn't take my advice!

Her ADHD husband: *I did come to her, but only with some questions about how to set up the carpooling. And I was only asking if she would back me up, which she ought to be willing to do.*

All of these couples exhibit parenting and child-like behaviors. The first woman "needs" her husband's therapist to know certain things and is looking for ways to make sure this happens. The second correctly identifies that her husband is acting like a child—he's using her for functions that he ought to be taking responsibility for but isn't. Note that she participates in parenting behaviors such as making him lists, anyway. The third couple's carpooling problems capture both parenting and child-like dependence. She gave him instructions and then he did it his own way—yet didn't take responsibility for this choice. Instead, he circled back to her for ideas and support. Parent figures "overfunction" and step outside of their own areas of responsibility to take on those of their partner. The "child" partner "underfunctions," reinforcing the other partner's parenting behavior.

This points out something very important about parent/child dynamics. *Both partners are often complicit.* It's too easy for ADHD partners to blame more organized partners for being controlling. Yet ADHD partners play into the dynamic by not fully taking charge of themselves. This is yet another reason why optimizing treatment is so important. Good treatment allows ADHD partners to stand on their own two feet in the relationship. And developing a stronger sense of where your own boundaries are can help keep you from over or under-functioning.

Moving away from parent/child dynamics starts with identifying parent/child behaviors and responding in specific ways. Here are some basic guidelines for starting this process:

- **When you say you will be fully in charge of something, take *full* responsibility for it from beginning to end.** The man setting up the carpooling should have asked questions of the other people in the carpool. If he had done so, he would have gotten more relevant answers. After all, they were directly involved. For her part, the wife could have acknowledged (i.e., validated) her husband's right to do the carpooling his way (remember, he's in charge!) and just politely reminded him that she wasn't free to be his backup driver—he would need to solve the problem another way.
- **If it has to do with doctor/patient relationships, you are only in charge of your own relationships.** If you think your partner could do something better in therapy, feel free to voice that in a respectful way, but that's as far as it should go. It's his therapy and his body. The same goes for medication choices and management.
- **Making lists for someone else is usually a form of parenting** and remaining in control. More organized partners should transition away from this behavior unless it is part of your agreed-upon way of interacting for specific projects (i.e., everyone is pleased with the arrangement). Note that *coordinating* responsibilities is not the same thing as parenting.
- **Nagging always indicates parenting behavior.** It means taking responsibility for someone else's time deadline and follow-through.
- **Creating consequences is also parenting behavior.** Consequences should naturally fall out of whatever each of you is doing—they don't need to be created.
- **If you are relying on your partner for everyday functioning,** you are in a child posture in the relationship.

- **If you are constantly giving a partner advice** about how to do things, or critiquing whether or not he or she did things the right way, you are parenting. Furthermore, you are probably setting yourself up for additional frustration. ADHD partners don't do things the same way non-ADHD partners do.

Setting and Respecting Boundaries

Strengthening your own personal boundaries is an important part of living together successfully as a couple, particularly if ADHD is in the mix. In *The ADHD Effect on Marriage*, there is an entire chapter on why boundaries are important, how to reset your own boundaries, and one detailed example of doing so if you want more detail on this topic.

For the purposes of this discussion, boundaries are a way of learning to say no *to yourself* primarily, or to your partner when it makes sense for you personally to do so. When you set boundaries and say to your partner, "I will no longer overfunction; therefore I will no longer take on so much of your work." A short-term result may be that the ADHD partner will underfunction even more. With no one reminding him or her of the chore she's gotten distracted from…you know the rest of this story. But as painful as that may be, the long-term result of doing the opposite—of *not* saying "no"—is *worse* than that. The short-term pain of more underfunctioning must be endured and then negotiated in all the ways we outline in this book in order to get to the longer-term goal of a happy, balanced relationship. When non-ADHD partners cover up or take on an unreasonable proportion of the responsibilities to accommodate ADHD problems, those problems last longer because some of the pressure to fix the issues is lessened. Further, the resentment that builds between partners as the overfunction/underfunction pattern continues becomes deeper and more troublesome.

Non-ADHD partner: *When I say, "We need help with managing ADHD," he says, "Don't worry about me. I'll deal with it." Is it possible that my husband can successfully manage his ADHD all on his own?*

Here's that fear again, the fear that a less organized, ADHD partner can't do it without help. So "help" is offered in a number of ways—instructions, education, nagging, the creation of support structures such as lists and the creation and maintenance of consequences. The non-ADHD partner becomes the manager or police person in the relationship.

These feelings of fear often come from a long history of prior ADHD partner behavior. But it isn't that the ADHD partner can't be reliable. It's that he or she has great difficulty being consistent without good treatment and structures. Non-ADHD partners must fight hard against their desire to control and help out...it's not their body, even though undermanaged ADHD symptoms greatly impact them. Concurrently, ADHD partners must fight hard to manage their ADHD. The result of either partner's unwillingness to participate will be a relationship that fails to thrive.

It most certainly is possible for most adults to manage their ADHD, though we urge non-ADHD partners to remember that their ADHD partner may not function in the same way that they do. With treatment, ADHD partners will likely get from point A to point B more consistently, but it will still probably not happen in a straight line! That's not a bad thing, by the way. Sometimes the journey is more interesting when it's less efficient. This is a lesson that Melissa has learned over time. In fact, she feels her life is enriched by the fact that she has been forced to become more patient as well as more thoughtful about restricting her role as family "manager."

In codependency speak, this process of learning to say no is called detachment. Not only do you accept the premise that other people's problems are not yours to solve, but you also come to accept that worrying doesn't help. You simply let people be who they are, giving them, as Beattie says, "The freedom to be responsible and grow."

The Enforcer Parent

> ***More organized ADHD partner:*** *I really don't want to be caught up in the parent/child cycle. However, I feel that there need to be consequences if there are boundaries. But that puts me right back into the parent role again. How do you have boundaries without consequences? Or how do you have consequences without crossing back into parent/child dynamics?*

To paraphrase Isaac Newton, for every action there is a natural reaction. You don't have to manufacture consequences… they just happen. We believe that it is the responsibility of the non-ADHD or more organized partner, *when contributing his or her best self to the relationship,* to strive to make that reaction constructive. You don't *punish* your partner for not getting a task done on time—that would be parenting as well as counterproductive for the longer-term health of the relationship. But if a *pattern* of "incompletes" persists, you could sit down and talk about how hard that is on you and negotiate ways of improving the situation. You should start with a complaint (rather than a criticism) and use the skills outlined in the communication chapter. If the ADHD partner can't "fix" the problem—or doesn't want to—then you negotiate a work-around.

We see many more instances of non-ADHD partners acting as enforcers than we do ADHD partners, but sometimes that is the case, as well. One such situation occurs in ADHD / ADHD relationships when one ADHD partner takes on the role of "parent" in the same way a non-ADHD partner might. Another situation is when an ADHD partner is so angry at the non-ADHD partner that the ADHD partner chooses to punish his or her partner in some way, perhaps going on strike and refusing to interact.

Don't end up as an enforcer. There is no place in a partnership between two equals for one partner to punish the other. Reach out and seek peace, or at least a negotiated plan of action, instead.

Parent/Child Dynamics Diminish You Both

Even though you are aware that parent/child interactions hurt your relationship, you will find that it remains very tempting for non-ADHD partners to try to impose helpful solutions on their partners. For example:

> **Non-ADHD partner:** *Do you have any suggestions about keeping a journal of activities my ADHD partner does for himself? We have been having arguments about this, and I have reached a point where I can't trust that he will do things (such as sleep, exercise, eat right, take Omega oil, etc.) regularly and consistently enough to help his brain functioning. His behavior is difficult to measure since we live apart, so I have asked him to keep a journal of his daily activities to discuss with me later. He resists, however, saying he's being treated like a child. I can see that. He says he will set reminders to himself and I have to trust him. But I can't at this point. I can't figure out any other way that is agreeable to both of us. He asks me to go and live with him if I have to see whether he is doing it or not, which I feel is very unreasonable. We both have our own lives to take care of, and I also have my son living with me.*

This woman is unwittingly participating in some pretty negative relationship behavior in her desperation for improvements in her partner's behaviors. Though she correctly identifies it as parenting behavior, she can't think of any other ideas to *create change*. She even states this when she says, "I can't figure out any other way that is agreeable to both of us." She doesn't realize that her partner has told her in no uncertain terms that what she is suggesting is in *no way* agreeable to *both* of them—only to her!

She misses the point. She CAN'T force him to change. She's not in charge of his behavior management—and never will be. It does not *matter* whether she sees a "solution" she thinks will work. Only he is in charge of what he does, or does not do, to improve ADHD symptom management. She needs to back off, reiterate her interest in change, perhaps give voice to her dreams of how great their future will be together once he is more reliable (as she is sure he will be one day) and hope she can inspire him to want to make the changes she seeks. By attempting to make him change, she is diminishing herself as both a person and a partner. Furthermore, she's encouraging him to dig in and resist her.

> ***Non-ADHD partner:*** *What would you recommend a spouse of an ADHD partner do if there are many comments that degrade, belittle, and attack you? An example scenario: I said, "I'll plan to get a sitter and go to the school fundraiser with you if you'll plan to be moderate in drinking." My ADHD partner responded, "Oh, loosen up and have fun. All the other parents will be drinking." At this point I'd like to respond, "But they don't all make asses of themselves when drinking and socializing." But, of course I don't say that. I try to set limits so I don't get resentful, embarrassed or angry. However, I often end up acting from a parent/child scenario since the usual response is defensive, belittling, and attacking. Help! I feel as if I've been rowing a boat and getting nowhere for many years.*

This comment, when it came to us, was actually about validation. The woman who wrote it was hoping her husband would listen to her request that he behave himself in a way that wouldn't embarrass her. She wanted him to drink less. However, the combination of how she voiced that request (very indirectly) and her controlling approach had the opposite effect. She views his response as defensive and belittling without seeing that her attempt to bribe him was also belittling. She is trying to address *her* unease by controlling *his* behavior.

This woman is working against herself. She needs to talk directly to her partner about her feelings. "I'm having real trouble dealing with the loud and aggressive behavior you exhibit when you drink and want to talk with you about it. You offended several people at the last party, and I worry that no one will want to invite us to join them at parties any more. Can we talk about what's going on?" In this way she owns that her embarrassment is her problem. She voices a complaint rather than a criticism. But she does not assume that he must fix it—he is, after all, in control of himself. At first, she simply sets out to learn why he thinks this is happening and see if there is room for negotiation.

Is The ADHD Partner Capable?

All of these examples show how parenting behavior turns people who were previously loving partners into overbearing figures in the relationship. It also demonstrates how behaving in this way tends to set you against each other as adversaries. Stepping in, as all "parent" figures do in parent/child dynamics, reinforces a very negative message to ADHD partners.

> ***ADHD partner:*** *Please talk about how codependency creates the illusion that the ADD partner is incapable of taking care of himself and how demeaning that can be.*

Being the "child" in a parent/child dynamic is awful. Here you are, an adult, and the person who is supposed to be your best supporter is telling you that you are incompetent and a failure. ADHD partners may be inconsistent, but the impact of parenting behavior goes beyond complaining about problems. *Parenting*—i.e., actively taking over part of the job that the ADHD partner is supposed to be doing, is a far cry from *observing* that you would like your partner to take responsibility for being a better partner.

The first implies permanent incompetence (and, in fact, extends the duration of the problem) while the second implies that competence can be obtained but is still elusive.

There is a world of difference between these two assumptions for *both* partners. Like everyone else, ADHD partners are more likely to take charge of becoming more reliable partners when they are in a supportive, encouraging environment. Non-ADHD partners are more likely to be supportive, even in the face of adversity, if they haven't convinced themselves that their partner is permanently incapable or disabled. They should consider that their partner needs to improve treatment and can continue to make improvements. And, as it happens, research suggests that this is the reality once you know you have ADHD *and have undertaken to optimally treat it.*

We italicize the last point to remind you of its critical importance. Some with ADHD thrive without treatment, but many don't. Nor do their relationships. But treatment entails more than just identifying ADHD and popping a pill to take care of it. ADHD partners will be most successful at transforming their lives and marriages if they really jump into the three legs of treatment. The alternative—denial that ADHD is an issue—usually ends badly indeed.

Enjoy Life in the Present Moment

Rebalancing power has a great deal to do with detaching from your partner enough so that you each have the freedom to stand on your own feet. It also has to do with detaching yourself from your past difficulties and your worries about the future. You control *neither* the past nor the future. So one form of taking control is becoming more comfortable with living in the present moment—the here and now.

It just so happens that living in the "now" is typically an ADHD partner's strength. Often, it doesn't come quite so easily to non-ADHD partners...but is still achievable with practice.

When you live in the present moment, you allow life to happen to you, rather than try to force it and control it. You acknowledge, then set aside, your regrets about your past and focus on today with a hopeful attitude towards tomorrow. You make the most of each day.

This may sound antithetical to the intentional relationship concept. It's not, though. When you create an intentional relationship, you are thoughtfully making decisions each day that fit into a framework you have created in order to act consistently with *your own* most important priorities. You are not just aimlessly reactive to everything around you, but focused on being the best you possible. At the same time, you are *not* attempting to manipulate your partner or the world around you—only your *own* immediate behavior. For most, this approach imparts calmness, clarity, and purpose instead of what used to be chaotic responses to stressful inconsistency.

Seek to appreciate the present and anchor yourselves in the idea that at any given time what you have is what's happening to you *right at that moment*. It's up to each of you to make the best of it.

Intentionally Reconnect

Re-establishing the boundaries between you as unique individuals and eliminating parent/child dynamics tends to leave a void. After all, you were connecting during your parent/child interactions; it just wasn't a positive experience for you. As you straighten that out, you will notice that you are both more independent of each other again—and that is good! But relationships are about connecting, not living independently side-by-side. So you will also likely wish to intentionally add back more positive interactions.

Ned Hallowell calls connection "the other Vitamin C"—a critical part of life that most of us don't get enough of. In his book *Connect*, he movingly reviews the science and philosophy of connecting to anything larger than ourselves. Such connections sustain us and make our lives feel well-lived.

As enthusiastic supporters of committed partnerships (whether official "marriages" or not—as far fewer people today feel beholden to that institution) we hope that one of the most important connections in your life will be your partner. There are many ways to create and strengthen partnership connections once you are ready to do so. Note that connections don't always need to be verbal. Some strong non-verbal connections include pride in family, the joy of quietly holding each other, doing a favor for a partner that shows you care, reaching for a partner's hand while on a walk, or a facial expression that shows pleasure in a partner's accomplishment.

We urge you to think about how you and your partner connect best and start to intentionally create more of *that*—whatever it is—in your relationship.

A Success Story in the Making

While we were writing this book, a non-ADHD partner wrote a post at www.adhdmarriage.com about how she and her husband were in the process of overcoming parent/child issues. Before they could get to this point, they had to hit rock bottom. In their case, that included a difficult separation. We include her unedited story here because it encompasses so much of what we've been writing about in this chapter.

The story is still a work in progress but shows all the signs of becoming a happy turn-around. Both partners are now engaged in building a better future and taking control of their own issues to ensure a stronger union. He is finally working harder to manage his ADHD, while she is tackling her codependency and anger. We hope that once their relationship is calmed they will take the next step and add back the loving interactions that make their partnership, and family of six, so special.

(Non-ADHD partner)

Hope for the Hopeless

I wanted to share a bit of my story and where I'm at for those of you who are where I have been and was just a short time ago.

If you look down at some of my previous posts you will see a lot of my frustration/anger with my spouse and the point of hopelessness that I was at. Things had gotten so bad that we separated 2 months ago. We have 4 children, and have been married 12 years, so the decision was not an easy one to make. At the point that we separated I was not sure what my spouse would do. I was fully prepared that he may decide to do nothing and that our marriage would sadly come to an end.

Like many of you, I have tried hundreds of different tactics over the last 12 years. From begging/pleading, to nagging, to encouraging, to demanding/yelling, you name it, I've done it. I read The ADHD Effect on Marriage *2 years ago and it was like reading the story of our lives. The bad thing was that my spouse was unwilling to read the book or to participate in any of the plans/techniques mentioned in the book, so while it was helpful, it didn't go anywhere.*

When we separated I made it clear to my spouse that he had 6 months to get things figured out. I told him that I was unwilling to live our lives the way we had been living for the last couple years, and that I refuse to be his mother any longer. I have pursued counseling on my side and allowed him to do whatever he thinks he needs to do on his end. I wrote him a letter with clear boundaries as to what I would/would not tolerate and we separated the finances for the time being.

I won't lie and say things have been easy or even close to it. My children (all 4 under 11) are missing their daddy, and I really am not loving being a single mom (while going to school full time). I am having to take a hard look at MYSELF and my contributions to this whole mess, which isn't fun either. I read and reread the book Codependent No More, *which I think anyone on here should read IMMEDIATELY, because if you're like me, the entire book is applicable to your situations.*

The first few weeks were horrible, adjusting to the new normal, dealing with being alone, all of the emotions still between us. But slowly things leveled out a bit. It has been extremely hard for me to let go of all of the things that I had previously taken care of for him. Most were out of fear of what would happen if I didn't do it, like making sure he filled/took his meds, making sure he got up for work, making sure he turned in paperwork, etc. I had to quit that all cold turkey. He has stumbled around quite a bit on things, and is not doing it perfectly, but slowly he is picking back up the things that I had taken from him for so long.

I realized (after reading Codependent No More*), that the reason I was doing so much rescuing and taking care of so many things for him was because I didn't trust him to take care of himself, that I thought he was incompetent. In the process, he came to believe the same thing, that he was incapable of taking care of himself. The result was little to no self-confidence or ability to believe in himself. We were both stuck in this cycle of dependence and reacting that was miserable for both of us and got us nowhere.*

The separation, while extreme, forced him to face the choice of either giving himself 100% to fixing what was wrong, or losing his family. The consequences were/are in his face daily, and he knows that if we don't figure this out and quit running from it, we will lose our marriage.

We started Melissa's class on October 1st, and it has been an awesome resource and way for us to talk about the issues that got us to where we are now. He is finally willing to look at his part in things, and not run away because he's overwhelmed or afraid that I'm saying it's all his fault. Melissa does a great job of keeping both partners accountable for their part in the process, and not blaming it on one or the other. She is very clear about saying that if things are to get any better you BOTH have to work on your actions/reactions.

We are still in the beginning stages of fixing our relationship, but for the first time in a long time I have faith that we can make it work, without me having to sacrifice my happiness and live the rest of my life as his mother instead of his wife. I just wanted to encourage everyone here that no matter how dark it seems, if you have two people willing to find a way to make it work, you can do it. The problem, I think, a lot of the time with ADHDers, is getting them to the place that they realize that this is NOT something that can just be blown over or ignored. It may take something extreme or serious enough that they sit up and take notice.

It was not until I was willing to admit the reality of our situation, and realize that I would be miserable for the rest of my life if things didn't change drastically, that I was brave enough to lay it all on the line and possibly lose my marriage. I am still struggling daily with my codependent habits and I know we're a long way from having things fixed, but I know that no matter what the outcome of this, I and my kids (and my husband) will be in a better place because of it.

You CANNOT live the rest of your life being responsible for another adult. No matter how hard you try, you will never be able to control them, and you will make yourself crazy and miserable in the process. Your spouse IS capable of taking responsibility for themselves and their own actions, but that will not happen until you step back and allow/force them to do so. You DESERVE peace, you DESERVE to be loved, and you DESERVE a partner, not another child.

I hope my story/progress helps someone, I know it helped ME to read anything that seemed to help other couples in my situation when I was at my lowest point. Sometimes you just need a nudge to get on the road to where you need to go.

Warmth, Intimacy and Feelings of Love

" 'All beginnings are lovely,' a French proverb reminds us, but intimacy is not about that initial 'Velcro stage' of relationships. It is when we stay in a relationship over time—whether by necessity or choice—that our capacity for intimacy is truly put to the test."

— Harriet Lerner

What is intimacy? It's tempting to think of it as sex and romance, and we hope to help you find more of that in your relationship. But intimacy is something deeper than that—it's the ability to be *all* of yourself in your relationship and to feel comfortable and heard. It's a shared connection between two people that can only be reached when each person is a strong enough "I" in the relationship. It's two completely unique people who choose, for whatever reason, to bring their own strengths and weaknesses to join with those of another person in an open and honest way.

This view of intimacy has some ramifications:

- We must understand and acknowledge both our strengths and our weaknesses, and recognize that both partners possess both strengths and weaknesses.
- We need to be in touch with our values and then act on those values—bringing our best selves to the relationship.

- We should not confuse "best" with "perfect." If we quest for perfection, we will never find the acceptance needed for intimacy.
- We need to engage with each other, rather than disengage.
- Any and all behaviors that create power imbalances in the relationship obstruct a couple's ability to build intimacy. Such behaviors include parent/child dynamics, defensiveness, stonewalling, and/or denial that either partner's issues impact the relationship.

When you think about it, this view of intimacy makes a lot of sense. When you are able to freely express yourself in all of your iterations, and your partner is able to hear and respond in a positively engaged way to your ups and downs, you have an intimate relationship.

We *also* hope you will find, in addition, a warm and fun relationship. Some of you will be feeling fairly good about each other and simply looking for ways to iron out a few wrinkles. For others, struggles in your relationship may lead to wondering if you will ever feel true love for your partner again. You might feel you *ought* to be together, yet you might not feel joy or happiness when you are. *Can our love be rekindled?* is an important, and often anxiety-ridden, question. Our honest answer, if you are asking this question, is *we don't know, but we hope so.*

We have worked with many couples impacted by ADHD who fell out of love, only to rediscover love again once they better understood the dynamics underlying their relationship and had steered it into calmer waters. We hope you will be one of them. We are constantly amazed and delighted at the hidden wells of affection that lie underneath all the turmoil. It's such a joy when couples summon the courage to reach out and be vulnerable with each other again and relocate what's been missing.

Struggling couples *miss* each other. Perhaps some of the bitterness you have gone through stems from feeling as if your experiences have robbed you of your best friend and lover. You want that person back! Though you've gone through too much for your love to ever feel as innocent as it once did, you can relocate those lovely warm feelings again and be stronger for the journey you've made.

HOT SPOT 19
I Can't Trust My Partner

> **Non-ADHD partner:** *We seem to have the same conversations over and over again. For example, we had a really constructive conversation not too long ago, and I thought we had agreed on how we would proceed. But when I approached my partner yesterday, he responded emotionally and said we hadn't agreed to that. It was like we were right back at the beginning. How do you get around that?*

This woman has trouble trusting her husband because ADHD symptomatic behaviors leave her life constantly up in the air. Decisions never seem to stick. Her husband, when asked about his response, said, "I interpret things differently from her, and later when she comes back to me, I don't remember all of the specifics of what we have talked about." Melissa asked him if he felt strongly that he needed to please his wife, to which he responded, "Yes, I do. She's put up with a lot…and sometimes that feeling is so strong that I just go along." This coping strategy works until he is approached later, doesn't remember the details of why he agreed, and the whole thing feels uncomfortable to him.

This is a common issue—ADHD partners wish to please their non-ADHD partner either out of guilt or a desire to avoid conflict. So they agree when they aren't sure they really do agree. But the result isn't pleasure for the non-ADHD partner. Rather, it's a long-term erosion of trust. Eventually, this couple will likely be able to move away from this pattern by following these steps:

- Discuss the long-term impacts of this particular behavior and why it's in their best interests to move out of this pattern.
- Discuss his feelings about his recent ADHD diagnosis so she better understands his feelings of guilt and his unwillingness to stand up for his opinions.
- Develop a routine for recapping their agreements and double-checking that he genuinely agrees at the end of a conversation. Consider writing brief notes to capture the most important agreements. This may be particularly critical if his agreements appear to be true for him in the moment but then seem to fade or not be remembered over time.

This is just one example of a pattern in which one partner, often the ADHD partner, makes a promise of some sort, and then doesn't follow through as expected. Here's another common one:

> **Non-ADHD partner:** *My partner promised me he would be home in time to take the kids so that I could get out of the house for my meeting. He says he left early, but once again he ended up late and I had to scramble. I just can't trust him anymore.*

The larger question is this: *with all of the inconsistency in ADHD-impacted relationships, how do you learn to trust your partner again? Isn't trust all about dependability?* Understanding more about the science of trust can help us answer these questions.

But before we get there, let's briefly revisit the idea of internal stories, first covered in Chapter 4, because the internal stories we tell ourselves have a huge impact on our ability to rebuild trust. As Gottman suggests, this is particularly true of the overarching story we tell ourselves about our partner's *character.*

If your internal story is positive in general *(my wife struggles with ADHD, but is a warm-hearted person),* you will likely be able to look past inconsistencies and conclude you can trust her to *do her best and to try to work in your mutual best interests*—even if the outcome isn't always what you want. That internal story allows you to let some of the results of ADHD behaviors pass by you, rather than stick like a burr. If your internal story is more negative (*my wife rarely does anything right*), you are more likely to conclude that you can't trust her and so must keep tabs on her mistakes.

And, to turn things around, if you are a partner with ADHD and your internal story is negative (*my wife always thinks I'm incompetent and never supports me*) you are less likely to place your trust in her to try her best to treat you well than if your story is positive (*my wife has my best interests at heart, even if she gets frustrated sometimes*). You might be more likely to assume she's judging you than that she's trying to stay connected when she talks with you.

We urge you to repeatedly question the veracity of your internal stories and push to make sure they are as positive as makes sense for your situation. Positive stories can aid you as you look to rebuild trust for each other.

The Elements of Trust...Plus ADHD

As you seek to thrive in your relationship, it will help if you understand some of the science behind rebuilding trust. Again, John Gottman's research provides key insights. In his in-depth book, *The Science of Trust: Emotional Attunement for Couples,*

Gottman delineates two dimensions of trust that concern many couples (Gottman, 2011, p. 177):

1. **Transparency:** The opposite of lying and deceit. Transparency is all about keeping promises and being truthful in the relationship.
2. **Positive moral certainty:** Knowing that your partner is a moral, ethical person. This element of trust delineates how you think your partner will treat you—with respect, integrity, kindness and good intentions.

We suspect you are already considering these two elements and bumping them up against the experiences you have had in your ADHD-impacted relationship. You may well see the challenges that *undiagnosed or undermanaged* ADHD symptoms added to maintaining trust in your partnership. Think back to the time before you knew about ADHD. The ADHD partner agreed to do something, but then got distracted and didn't follow through on that promise. This happened over and over again, and led to the chore wars and parent/child dynamics. For many couples, trust eroded even before they knew about ADHD.

We hope that ADHD symptoms are now being well enough controlled that ADHD doesn't interfere as much as it used to. But we recognize that symptoms rarely disappear completely. An ADHD partner will *never* become *non-ADHD*. We strongly believe that accepting this reality is a critical component of thriving in an ADHD-impacted relationship. This has some implications when you talk about trust.

> **Non-ADHD partner:** *I am disturbed to hear you talk about being flexible with ADHD partners who break their promises. To me, marriage is all about keeping your promises. We're spouses. If we make a promise, it should be kept. ADHD shouldn't be some sort of excuse that gets the ADHD partner off the hook when he changes his mind or doesn't do something.*

While we agree with the sentiment this woman expresses, we take a pragmatic view of the topic. The very symptoms that define ADHD mean that, at least some of the time, an ADHD partner will probably not fulfill his or her promises. Because of this, we believe that the intent *and actions* taken to support that intent are really important. Your partner may have failed, but did he do everything possible to fulfill that promise? Is treatment supporting the eventual goal of being reliable enough? Has the couple developed a way to communicate about an impending broken promise? We think it's realistic to expect that some commitments will be broken when ADHD is in the picture...but that doesn't necessarily make ADHD partners untrustworthy.

You can develop a relationship in which you know, 100% of the time, that both partners will act with the utmost respect, integrity and good intentions towards each other. In this situation, the equation for rebuilding trust becomes modified like this (our changes in italics):

1. **Transparency:** The opposite of lying and deceit. Transparency is all about keeping promises *to the best of your ability* and being truthful in the relationship. *It means operating with complete openness about, and ownership of, all positive and negative events.*
2. **Positive moral certainty**: Knowing that your partner is a moral, ethical person. This element of trust delineates how you think your partner will treat you—with respect, integrity, kindness and good intentions.
3. ***Empathy and understanding of ADHD:*** *In-depth knowledge about ADHD symptoms and how they present in your relationship; an appreciation for the difficulties ADHD poses for both of you*

Rebuilding trust just looks different for couples impacted by ADHD. Difficulty with follow-through means ADHD partners may struggle to consistently fulfill the commitments underlying the transparency side of the trust equation—even with the best intentions and, sometimes, the best treatment. This means that couples cannot put as much emphasis on task completion as they might like to. The idea that *my partner's got my back* must rely on emotional factors more heavily than logistical ones. So, for example, in Nancie and Steve's marriage, even when his follow-through is far from perfect, she is well aware that his intentions are always good and honorable; she knows he always has their mutual best interests at heart (and vice versa). This has been a cornerstone for the trust in their relationship.

Yes, we are suggesting you modify the typical conditions for maintaining trust in your partnership specifically because ADHD is present. Your relationship is *not* like the average relationship, and to base your ability to trust your ADHD partner upon his or her ability to fulfill all obligations on time, every time, is a fool's errand. On the other hand, the ADHD partner who does not do his or her *utmost* to manage ADHD symptoms has not, in our opinion, earned the right to expect this modification. ADHD may be a *reason* that one cannot always follow through. It should never be an *excuse* for not trying your hardest to do so.

Rebuilding trust must become part of that intentional relationship we've referred to. It won't just happen. Couples need to:

- Do their absolute best to avoid rashly committing to obligations they cannot fulfill
- Coordinate their expectations
- Do their utmost to fulfill all obligations to which they do commit, understanding that sometimes ADHD will still get in the way
- Think about how they fight, and engage only in "good fights" so each person knows that his or her partner will not aggressively attack

- Consciously turn *toward* their partner and listen when he or she expresses a complaint, rather than turn away
- Keep each other aware of issues and feelings about patterns (versus individual incidents) rather than hide them
- Listen in a non-defensive way
- Ensure they have a partner's full attention before talking about *anything* important
- Consistently validate their partner and do everything possible to even out the power that each partner has—avoiding parent/child interactions at all costs
- Get ADHD symptoms under control so they can improve consistency and so they have the mental bandwidth to be responsive to their partners in daily interactions. Optimizing ADHD treatment is critical to building ADHD reliability and success in the relationship.

HOT SPOT 20
I Don't Feel Connected

Most of us suffer from not getting enough time to connect. The pace of our incredibly busy lives means we work longer hours and see each other less. When we are together, tasks hang over our heads and our smart gadgets draw our attention away from the people around us. What's more, our kids have schedules that are as demanding as our own.

Oh, yeah. And then we add ADHD.

If you are feeling disconnected from your spouse, you are certainly not alone. And ADHD is only part of the issue. Getting reconnected is one of the main goals of living in an intentional relationship. Happily, marriage research can help us find relatively efficient ways to get there.

Activities That Connect You

In *The ADHD Effect on Marriage,* Melissa reviewed research done by Arthur Aron, a professor of psychology at Stonybrook University. Aron's work suggests that when couples partake in "new and challenging" activities together, they not only have fun but also start to associate some of the exhilaration of the experience with their partner.

Aron hypothesizes that the connection boost couples get when doing new and challenging things together has to do with self-expansion. "We enter relationships because the other person becomes part of ourselves, and that expands us," Dr. Aron is quoted as saying in the *New York Times* (Parker-Pope, 2010). "That's why people who fall in love stay up all night talking and it feels really exciting. We think couples can get some of that back by doing challenging and exciting things together."

"Opposites attract" may be one expression of this idea of self-expansion. When a logical, organized non-ADHD partner meets a spontaneous, energetic ADHD partner, sparks fly. They add so much to each other's world! This concept, taken one step further, also provides insight into why the differences between you can become real assets in your relationship—provided ADHD symptoms don't get in the way. We'll explore that idea later in this chapter.

"New and Challenging" Things to Do Together

- Take up white water rafting
- Take tango lessons
- Rent rollerblades or cross-country skis
- Climb a local mountain
- Volunteer at a soup kitchen
- Enter a Lego building contest
- Write/illustrate a children's book for your kids
- Design and build a garden
- Go to a convention on a topic you know nothing about
- Run a 10K
- Go on a bike tour together
- Go geocaching
- Camp on the beach and cook out
- Do yoga
- Take a gourmet cooking class, or any other class that intrigues you

Another concept useful for connecting is "flow." This is a concept developed by Mihaly Csikszentmihalyi that asserts that our ability to become fully immersed in a meaningful activity ("flow") is what makes us happy. In a 2004 TED talk, he described flow as such complete immersion that one loses touch with one's body, time disappears, and you are part of something larger. You do the activity for its own sake, to your own heart's content.

"Flow" happens when challenges are harder than average and skills are higher than average. You can move yourself into flow by choosing to undertake challenging tasks and matching your skillset to that task. Some new and challenging activities may do this for you as a couple. Ideas include dance, meditation, making music, playing tennis, making love, playing video games, riding bikes, attending religious services or praying, and practicing yoga. If you become good enough to reach a state of flow, it will add to your sense of well-being.

We have written elsewhere about scheduling time to be together. We urge you to think about flow and "new and challenging" activities as you contemplate what you will do together. This can help build your connections and feelings of love.

Reconnection Fears

While you long to reconnect, you may harbor fears about doing so, as well. *What if warming up the relationship communicates that all is well and my partner stops working so hard on her ADHD? Will hugging and kissing my partner indicate that his criticisms of me are acceptable?* These are just two of a number of fears that partners secretly hold on to as they contemplate taking the actions that will better connect them. Unfortunately, that fear may keep you from making progress. While waiting for things to look more perfect—more ready for connection—you miss opportunities to connect, thus working against your goal of an improved relationship.

We suggest you take the opportunity to examine the filters you've developed. If your mindset is that *I just can't risk getting hurt anymore,* then you will have difficulty moving in a new direction. If, instead, your mindset is one of forward movement *(Connection starts by reaching out to my partner. I can't risk NOT trying to connect),* then you will likely create more opportunities for connection. If you do not reach out, reconnecting may be slow. If you do reach out, you may be able to connect or you may not, but your chances will be improved.

We are not suggesting that you should reach out at all costs. Reaching out when faced with consistent rejection, anger or abuse is not wise. We simply suggest you inspect whether your fears are well enough founded to risk *not* reaching out.

Giving, Connection and Rejection

"Giving is contagious. When you give genuinely and consistently, your partner will give back." These or similar words are fairly standard romance advice. The problem is that in ADHD-impacted relationships, they aren't always true. You can give of yourself greatly—really focus on being kind and thoughtful—and all that happens is your partner's life gets easier, while your own becomes all the more filled with problems.

This happened to Melissa when she tried to test George's hypothesis that her anger—and *not* George's ADHD—was the real problem in their relationship. What would happen if she was really, really nice instead? So for a month or more she would do everything she possibly could for him, and be as nice as possible. The result was not good. George was delighted—his life was suddenly wonderful…and he merrily went on with his life as always. If anything, he paid even less attention to Melissa than he had when she was angry and pursuing him. Melissa, who was at first hopeful, ended up feeling stifled and unable to take the humiliation of his continued disinterest. Here she was, as nice as she possibly could be, and George *still* paid her zero attention. The expression of his ADHD symptoms—which felt like rejection—was stunningly painful. She tried this twice. The first time she didn't announce what she was doing. The second, she told him what she was doing and asked that he try to respond back to her efforts. But because he wasn't managing his ADHD symptoms, the result was the same both times. He lost track of her, and at the end of each experiment she was angrier than she had been at the beginning.

As you try to build connections in your relationship, make sure it's genuinely a joint effort. One of you will always have to lead, so don't sit back and wait for your partner to be ready, but do make sure your connection efforts are joint and the ADHD partner is actively working to attend. That doesn't just mean trying harder to pay attention. Trying harder doesn't last. It means trying *differently* and optimizing treatment with all of the many ideas about what works for those with ADHD. Don't set yourself up for rejection by making a long-term, one-sided stab at connection.

Criticism and Sexual Connection

Sex, of course, is an important form of connection. A fair number of couples with whom we work have not had sex for months, sometimes years. (This may be the result of self-selection—the lack of sex sends them to seek help.) One couple with whom Melissa worked had not had sex for well over a year. They still loved each other, and the non-ADHD wife was wildly interested in rekindling their sex life. Her husband wanted to improve their relationship, and liked foreplay, but was afraid that she would think critically of him during sex. No matter how she tried to engage him, his fear was so strong that he simply could not make love to her. It was a sadly reinforcing cycle. His fear of her critique kept him from having intercourse with his wife. Their lack of sexual intimacy made her more and more unhappy and critical.

This is only one of many examples we have heard from ADHD partners that the "constant critique" of their ADHD behaviors—even at low levels—impacts their ability to be sexual with their partners. Since sexual intimacy is usually a big part of connection, this has a huge impact on how partners feel about each other. Ask yourselves whether or not you are in this situation. If you are, take immediate steps to stop the critique. Your ability to be connected with each other is much more important than whether or not something is done "just right."

HOT SPOT 21
Sexual Relationship Problems

It's not a huge surprise that over the course of a multi-year relationship, sex with the same partner can get a bit stale. Statistics about the frequency with which couples have sex demonstrate that while couples, on average, have more sex than single people, the number of times they have sex over the years shows a steady pattern of decline (Parker-Pope, 2010, p. 80). But many couples impacted by ADHD find that they encounter far more difficult issues than boring familiarity. Parent/child dynamics, anger, criticism, medication side effects, chaos and sheer exhaustion are just a few of the issues that can dramatically alter your sex life for the worse. Since a lack of an intimate sexual connection usually results from, or results in, unhappiness with the relationship as a whole, couples need to reconnect intimately if they are to thrive.

Since your sex life typically reflects the overall health of your partnership, strengthening the foundation of your relationship is an important element of improving your sex life. That means, once again, focusing on the basics—good treatment for ADHD symptoms, learning to listen to each other well, and getting out of very unromantic parent/child dynamics, among other things. But there are other things you can do to improve your sex life, too.

Different Reasons for Having Sex

In research done by Elaine Hatfield et. al., men and women describe different reasons for wanting to have sex. Women tend to think of sex as "person oriented." In other words, they see sex as a way to express affection in their relationship. Men generally have a "body oriented" view of sex, with the goal being sexual satisfaction. It's not that men never want caressing or seduction —according to research reported by Parker-Pope, about 40% of men said they also want this. But a full 60% say they want their wives to be aggressive, without inhibition, and to ask directly for sex. These divergent views of sex create a natural conflict for many couples.

> ***Non-ADHD woman:*** *My issue is sex. It's important to me but not to him. From month one of marriage when I asked*

what was wrong, he always made up something: I changed, he didn't want me anymore. To him sex is a once a week release, nothing close or intimate. No physical affection at any other point during the week. Is there a way to get around this?

Non-ADHD woman: *I'm not interested in having sex with my partner right now. Our relationship needs to improve drastically and trust has to be restored before I will even think about having a sexual relationship with him. My ADHD spouse has a hard time understanding my need for trust to be restored and for his ADHD symptoms to be under better control before I can even consider sex. Second, in addition, he thinks viewing porn should be okay and I should talk to him about it. I am unable to even consider his viewing porn, especially since he so recently has lost my trust with a second affair. I am afraid I won't be able to forgive him and/or trust him enough to maintain our marriage.*

Neither of these women is having sex, but neither of them reports they lack libido. They are simply having a difficult time reconciling their feelings about what sex ought to be with what has actually happened in their relationships. Some of this is a straight male/female split about what sex is all about and has nothing to do with ADHD. But some of it is very much about ADHD. Notice the first woman's comment that her husband said she had "changed" and he didn't want her any more. Chances are good that he was feeling the sting of her actions towards him (Disapproval? Parenting? Critiquing? Anger? Resentment?). He has chosen the coping strategy of withdrawing from her.

The second relationship has been dysfunctional for so long that the husband has sought sexual release elsewhere. His wife has not recovered from this betrayal.

The Sex-Starved Marriage

In her book *The Sex-Starved Marriage,* Michele Weiner-Davis tackles relationships like these, in which one partner wants sex more often than the other. She, too, cites the gap between women's emotionally-centered approach to sex and men's body-centric approach. But she adds another twist. Women typically want to connect emotionally *before* having sex whereas men often want to have sex in order to feel connected *afterward.* Her net take is that the issue is not *why* a couple isn't having sex, but rather that they *aren't* having sex.

To start to move forward again, try internalizing the following idea, crystalized so clearly by Pat Love in the foreword to *The Sex-Starved Marriage* (Weiner-Davis, 2003, foreword):

> "Even if no or little sex is not a problem for *you*, you *still* have a problem in your marriage. Far too many couples live with an unspoken, unworkable contract that goes something like this: *'I expect you to be monogamous, but don't expect me to meet your sexual needs.'"*

This sounds an awful lot like the woman who is now dealing with unwanted porn in her marriage.

We won't sugarcoat this problem. Getting sex going again is tough once you've gotten out of the habit, or once hard feelings have interfered. But not having sex is a recipe for disaster in your relationship. It leaves the partner who wants more sex feeling lonely and abandoned...something you do *not* need on top of all of the other issues you face while trying to stay connected in your ADHD-impacted relationship!

Weiner-Davis' book tackles this issue in far more depth than we could possibly do here. If you struggle with a sex life that either of you feels is not satisfying, we suggest you might benefit from reading it.

Sex and ADHD Symptoms

Some ADHD partners tell us they become easily bored during sex. Being with the same partner doesn't stay "shiny" for long. Others struggle to stay focused during sex. One woman with ADHD memorably noted, "If the dog barks, that's it! I'm so distracted the sex is basically over!" Not only does this make sex less pleasant for the partner with the ADHD, but it also impacts a non-ADHD partner's willingness to engage with his or her ADHD partner:

> **Non-ADHD partner:** *My main problem with sex is his distractibility and lack of positive touches/communication leading up to sex. Most weeks I have to admit that I would rather clean the toilets than pretend again to be into sex. This cycle truly needs to be broken. Any ideas?*

Distractibility and boredom are enemies to good sex, which is all about attention—both in the bedroom and outside of it. So these topics are worthy of conversation between you to see if you can gain better understanding. Is it simply ADHD symptoms that are appearing? In this situation, Dr. Hallowell suggests that taking a short-acting ADHD medication between 30 minutes and 3 hours before you have sex might solve the problem. (Note: this means that you would have to move your sex life to an early enough time that the medication wouldn't interfere with the ADHD partner's sleep.) Is exhaustion a factor? Or schedules? Perhaps one is a night owl and the other is an early riser? If this is the case, weekend afternoons might be ripe for setting aside time to have sex together.

Boredom can be addressed by adding new elements to your sex life at regular intervals. This can include changing where and when you have sex and/or adding sex toys, erotic materials, new types of foreplay, or role-playing. You may also wish to incorporate risk (will you get caught having sex outdoors?), seduction, or anything else that appeals and is safe and agreed upon by both partners. A word of warning on seduction, though: beware setting yourself up for rejection. If your issue is deep, as was the case for the man who feared criticism, no amount of seduction will work. In that case you likely would need the assistance of a professional therapist. So we're suggesting seduction for couples that already have a sex life as one way to decrease boredom and minimize distraction.

For those looking for sex and romance refreshers, or to broaden their horizons, there are some good resources available. Two that combine sexual therapy credentials with a variety of ideas and formats are Dr. Ruth Westheimer's book *Rekindling Romance for Dummies* and the Sinclair Institute website and materials, such as their *The Better Sex Guide*. We also like the supportive environment of the website www.babeland.com for women looking to find out what sex toys are all about for the first time.

Sex and Physiology

Sometimes, disinterest in sex is biological. Many factors can contribute, including:

- Changing hormonal levels in menopause
- Low levels of testosterone
- Medications, particularly antidepressants and contraception
- Nutritional problems
- Alcohol use
- Tobacco use
- Health problems that interfere with sex
- Exhaustion

If you feel too blah to have sex, or feel one of these might be a factor in your relationship, you might try any of these:

- Set a sleep schedule that reduces exhaustion
- Have sex first thing in the morning, when male testosterone levels are at their peak
- Stop drinking alcohol for a while and see what happens
- Talk with a doctor about switching medications to see if it helps
- Consider therapies that might lessen menopausal symptoms

And, of course, talking with your doctor about your specific issue might help.

Adding That Spark: Re-finding Love and Romance

Let's say that you're feeling good about the more fruitful ways you interact with each other, and are gaining confidence that ADHD symptoms really can be managed in your relationship. You've started to have sex again more often, and warm feelings are returning.

Now what?

Whether you are still searching for romantic inspiration or are just looking for a tweak, we would like to share some ideas about romance and ADHD that we think are relevant.

What Drives You Crazy... and What You Love

Romance is encouraged when partners are thrilled by their significant others...or at least excited by who they are. This can come in so many ways—the thrill of having your partner "attend" to you; the attractive wiggle of his behind as he walks down the hall; the way her hair smells; pride in her success at publishing her first research study or running her first road race; excitement when he gets a challenging new opportunity at work. Romance is stronger when partners feel good about themselves.

But romance can falter when you focus on a partner's—or your own—shortcomings, and too often these shortcomings are associated with the label of ADHD. Think back to those perception filters we discussed in Chapter 4. Now think about the words you associate with ADHD. They probably include words such as distracted, impulsive, hyperactive, forgetful, disorganized, stubborn, and inconsistent. Are we right? These are the words that are widely associated with ADHD in the media, in books (including this one), at the doctor's office and, chances are, in your home. They are fairly negative and hard to get positively (romantically) excited about.

But let's remove that filter for a moment and think differently. What would you say if your partner were curious, creative, energetic, able to get completely into what he is doing, spontaneous, persistent, and a person who showed great flashes of brilliance? Hmmm! Sounds a lot more interesting.

In their book *SuperParenting for ADHD*, Peter Jensen and Dr. Ned Hallowell argue that this second list includes the "mirror traits," or positive side, of ADHD symptoms. What is curiosity, for example, but showing an interest in everything around you? Sounds a lot like distraction.

It just so happens that the mirror traits of ADHD line up very nicely with what non-ADHD and other-ADHD partners tell us they love about their ADHD spouses. In a writing assignment on the topic in Melissa's couples' seminar, partners of ADHD spouses say (among other things) that they love that their partners are creative, spontaneous, able to enjoy the moment, visionary, totally focused when they are in the zone, fun, easy-going, persistent, energetic, passionate, and more. These descriptions are, essentially, Hallowell and Jensen's list of mirror traits!

We would argue, in fact, that ADHD characteristics are one of the reasons you were attracted to your partner in the first place. Though you have since learned that ADHD symptoms can sometimes create problems, to view them *only* as a source of difficulty is to cut yourselves off from an area of great strength in your relationship—the ability to recognize and celebrate ADHD characteristics. Hallowell likes to call ADHD a "gift that is hard to unwrap." He is careful to acknowledge that it is a gift that comes with strings attached. But there is much to learn from his approach to thinking about ADHD as a positive factor in your lives! In fact, it can breathe life into your quest for finding that thrill again in your partnership.

We would also like to point out that the very characteristics that drive ADHD partners crazy in their non-ADHD partners are also those with which they fell in love and can love again. In the same writing assignment, ADHD partners tell us that they love that their partners are organized, clean, think about everything, able to calm others down, loyal, supportive, caring, giving, and more. Again, if ADHD partners only see the downside of "organized" and "think about everything," then they lose out. Why not appreciate the fact that your partner "has a gift for organizing"? It won't change each partner's responsibility to take care of him or herself, but the positive mindset will make it easier to become more romantically interested.

Before we move on, we do not want you to stereotype "ADHD" and "non-ADHD." You are different, in general, but are not just your ADHD or non-ADHD qualities. Here are just a few of the words that were written about *both* ADHD and non-ADHD partners in that same writing assignment: focused, funny, sensitive, romantic, dedicated, compassionate, generous, smart, devoted, and loving.

A&A: Appreciation and Action

You will add joy in your relationship simply by increasing the amount of appreciation you show your partner. If you can't remember to do that because you are easily distracted, create a game with yourself to remember. Or perhaps hang a reminder note on your mirror about appreciation. Experiment until you find a system that reminds you to tell your partner something that you appreciate about him or her every single day.

But here's a trick for ADHD partners who are thinking about rekindling romance. Add to that appreciation some action—specifically, action *that your partner requests.* The action he or she chooses might not sound at all appealing to you. That's okay—you're trying to woo your partner, not yourself! We've had quite a few women tell us that they started thinking more warmly towards their spouse when he started doing the dishes! Men have a hard time understanding this. Trust us when we say you don't have to *understand* this. Just ask your partner what you could do, then figure out how to *do* it. Words are very meaningful. But when you've been married to a person with ADHD for a long time, actions are even more important—perhaps because it's clear by then how much energy and effort some of those actions take.

Ditto non-ADHD partners. Show appreciation at every opportunity. Seek out opportunities to give your partner full credit for the hard work he or she is doing. And then add action—not what *you* think should happen, but what your *partner* requests.

A&A is a potent combination that improves your appreciation of each other and helps your partner remember the kind, giving person you are. It's a great way to build romantic feelings.

The Power of Gratitude

There is now a fairly large body of psychology research concerning the impact that positive thought and action have to improve our lives. You can use some of this knowledge to find satisfaction, love and romance in your relationship.

One of the most helpful lessons from positive psychology is that gratitude helps you improve your life and your health. It does this by changing your perceptions and interpretation of what is happening to you. For example, a couple may have struggled for 10 years. One way to view that is to focus on the many years of struggle. Alternately, while acknowledging that struggle, they can be *grateful* that they now have the strength and experience as a couple to make it through anything. Though the facts remain the same, the second interpretation of the couple's struggle provides a proactive and upbeat platform from which to attack their next problem and feel good about their relationship.

That is just one example of finding the positive in things you have formerly found difficult. Seeking to feel gratitude *in general* is also a powerful tool. One exercise we give our clients is to take a few minutes each day to think of three things for which they are grateful. They might journal about these things, share them with their family or spouse (for example, at the dinner table), or simply peruse them in their minds. You might write about your partner: *I'm grateful for the dimple on my husband's chin; for my wife's installation of the new mailbox today; for my husband's ability to find a new job.* You might also be grateful for things that have nothing to do with your partner: *I'm grateful for the feeling of the warm, summer rain on my shoulders as I walked down the street today; for my son's smile; for the holiday cookie tradition passed down from my grandmother*. Gratitude exercises like this one remind you of all that is *right* in the world around you, and the feeling you get from them extends to many parts of your life—improving your overall health, your mental health and even your sleep.

When you are seeking to find that special something in your relationship again, it's a great thing to be reminded that the world is actually a pretty good place and that your life can be, too.

Some Basics That Shouldn't Be Forgotten

Even though you are in a relationship impacted by ADHD, it is not all about ADHD and responses to ADHD. Sometimes it's just about life. When you are seeking to be more romantically interested in each other, here are some basic concepts that we often see couples forget:

- **Act kindly towards your partner.** Random, (and even not-so-random!) acts of kindness enhance the warmth of any relationship.
- **Give for the sake of giving** to another, not for the purpose of getting. A gift of kindness, attention or respect is given because it is the right thing to do in your relationship. Don't give in order to receive.
- **We love others best when we love ourselves.** Actively seek ways to appreciate all the gifts you bring to your relationship, while also truthfully owning your weaknesses. Love all of who you are. You deserve it.
- **We are responsible for our own happiness.** If you are dissatisfied with your life and who you are as a person, do something about it. Focus on finding your best self and giving more time and energy to the things that put a smile on your face. Let go of feelings that your partner is responsible for making you happy.
- **Certain periods of our lives are more stressful than others.** For example, having young children is extremely stressful. During this time, be kind to yourselves and don't blame either yourself or your partner for life-stage stress. Focus instead on what can be done to relieve the stressful situation in which you find yourselves.

- **Relationships matter most**. After you've reached the ability to survive financially and everyone is basically healthy, your relationship with your partner and family matter more than anything else. Strive to understand your partner's feelings and make choices that demonstrate your love.

Success Stories

Many couples impacted by ADHD can learn how to thrive together—we see it happen with regularity. So, in closing, we would like to leave you with the words of three people who have learned to thrive in their ADHD-impacted relationships. We hope that you, too, will end up feeling as if you have found a deep and lasting love.

"What I'm most excited about is that I have my best friend back again!"

"It is remarkable that after (implementing the ideas you recommended) our marriage situation changed from 'the worst' to 'the best' in only 8 months! We will continue our effort to improve, but I can say confidently that our marriage is 'happily staying'...Oh, before I forget, last but not least, our sex life that was the equivalent to something like a 80 year old couple got better as well!"

"Yesterday we celebrated 29 years since we fell in love, but now I feel that the love we have recommitted to since (starting to work on this) is true, mature, lasting, 'til death do us part kind of love. I feel empowered that we can make it through anything as a couple, whereas in the past, we made it through things as separate units. And for this Valentine's Day my husband is actually taking me dancing—who knew?!"

We wish you all the best in your search for a healthy, joyous, and deep appreciation of the gifts that you offer each other.

Want to Learn More?

The vast majority of the questions quoted in this book were asked of Melissa in her couples' seminar. This is a multi-session course she gives by teleconference (and in a recorded version, for those who prefer to take it at their own pace). The course is an outstanding resource that has helped many struggling couples turn their relationships around. Information about how you can participate can be found at www.adhdmarriage.com.

We urge couples interested in improving their ADHD-impacted relationship to visit the www.adhdmarriage.com website. It is simply the best, most comprehensive resource available today to help couples learn how to manage ADHD and responses to ADHD. At the site you will find advice, free resources, books, seminars, information about the latest research and treatment for adult ADHD, referrals information, and a community of people facing the same issues you face. In short, you will find the support you need as you work to create a relationship in which you can both thrive.

We also encourage you to send your counselor to the therapist section of the website if he or she wishes to learn more. Counselors can find information about therapist training, research, therapist consultations, and more.

You are invited to stay in touch. Melissa can be reached through the contact form at www.adhdmarriage.com and Nancie can be reached at www.transformurlife.com.

For more information, visit

www.adhdmarriage.com

Worksheet and Additional Information

Two-Day Validation Tracking Worksheet

For two days, note and rate every response you have toward each other. To do this well, you'll need to sit down about once an hour and think about your interactions during that hour. A "1" is a wonderful interaction that validated you or your partner; a "5" is an interaction that completely invalidated one of you. Any time you have an interaction, good or bad, write it down. Track your own behavior as well as your spouse's. This goes both ways.

Any of the following earn an automatic 5:

- Criticism
- Contempt
- Stonewalling
- Sarcasm
- Defensiveness
- Criticism masked as "help"

Paying no attention (for whatever reason) should also be noted in the poorer end of the spectrum (you can figure out later if it was due to the ADHD symptom of distraction or an intentional putdown).

At the end of the experiment, find some time to sit down together and talk about what you've discovered. There may be patterns, such as a non-ADHD spouse being particularly critical around the subject of not getting enough attention, in which case it's likely that many of the invalidating actions are centered around ADHD symptom responses. There may be areas of strength that you need to note, as well.

Our hope is that this exercise will do three things for you:

1. Make you more aware of the frequency of destructive, invalidating behavior so you can diminish its presence in your lives.

2. Get you thinking about better, more validating, ways to respond in these same situations in the future.
3. Help you decide to reinforce existing validating interactions

You may find this exercise a bit depressing. But the first step in changing behaviors is identifying them.

Praise for Melissa Orlov's Couples' Seminar

"Your class had life-changing effects on our marriage. Thank you!"

"I took your course a year ago…I have been wanting to let you know that my husband and I are back together, very happily. It took me 5 trips out west, and the guts to follow my inner instincts, but in late August he drove back home. Your book and course were invaluable…Connecting with your work gave me the knowledge and courage to move forward in a positive way, even when things didn't look good…"

"We found out that there were so many couples like us. I can't tell you how good it feels to know that we are just normal people having a normal reaction to a difficult situation. We have made more progress in this seminar than we have in 2 years of couples therapy."

"I've really 'taken the bull by the horns' to try to beat this ADHD thing I have and know I can only work on myself. Thank you for empowering me when I hadn't felt empowered for a very long time!"

"Taking this course gave my husband and me the breakthrough we so desperately needed."

"This course offers precise, compassionate tools to create a marriage that is based on mutual trust and respect...Melissa speaks from her own experience and I am most grateful that she has taken the time to share this experience with us. I can honestly say that she has saved our marriage."

For more information about Melissa's couples' seminar, visit
www.adhdmarriage.com

Praise for Melissa Orlov and *The ADHD Effect on Marriage*

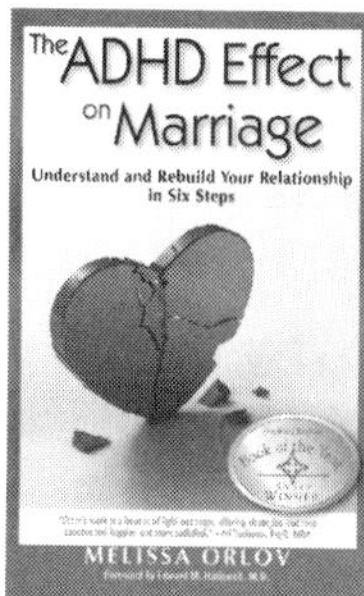

"Melissa Orlov is one of the foremost authorities on ADHD and relationships in the world today."

Dr. Edward Hallowell
Coauthor of *Driven to Distraction*
and many other books about ADHD

"If you are in a marriage affected by ADHD, this book is a must read for both spouses. Save yourselves years of pain and develop the loving marriage you both deserve by reading this book and applying the information Orlov shares from her heart."

Jonathan Scott Halverstadt, LMFT
Author of *ADD & Romance*

"Orlov's work is a beacon of light and hope, offering strategies that help couples feel happier and more satisfied."

Ari Tuckman, PsyD, MBA
Author of *More Attention, Less Deficit*

"*The ADHD Effect* is an exceptional book that addresses the complexity of the relationship between partners whose lives are affected by ADHD while presenting sound family system principles in an easy-to-understand and accessible way... I would highly recommend this book to my clients, their partners, and to couple therapists who want to learn to effectively guide couples in marriages challenged by *The ADHD Effect*."

Sari Solden, MS, LMFT
Author of *Journeys Through ADDulthood*

Audiobook available at www.adhdmarriage.com

References, Bibliography and Resources

Anand, M. (1989). *The art of sexual ecstasy: The path of sacred sexuality for western lovers*. New York, NY: Jeremy P. Tarcher/Putnam.

Fuses western and eastern love traditions for couples looking to broaden their sexual experiences with each other.

Anderson, J. (2013, February 17). Gluten and ADHD: Can a gluten-free diet help you manage attention deficit hyperactivity disorder? Retrieved from http://celiacdisease.about.com/od/commoncomplicationsofcd/a/Gluten-And-Adhd.htm

Attention deficit hyperactivity disorder. (2012). Retrieved from http://www.nimh.nih.gov/health/publications/attention-deficit-hyperactivity-disorder/index.shtml

Barkley, R. A. (2012, October). Effectiveness of restricted elimination diets for management of ADHD: Concerns about the 2011 INCA study. *The ADHD Report*, *20*(5), 1-12.

Barkley, R. A., & Benton, C. M. (2010). *Taking charge of adult ADHD*. New York, NY: Guilford Press.

Foremost ADHD researcher explains ADHD and provides advice about how to manage it. Full of facts and ideas.

Barkley, R. A., Murphy, K. R., & Fischer, M. (2008). *ADHD in adults: What the science says*. New York, NY: Guilford Press.

Methodologically rigorous review of the research on ADHD up to 2008.

Beattie, M. (1992). *Codependent no more: How to stop controlling others and start caring for yourself* (2nd ed.). Center City, MN: Hazelden.

The classic book from which to learn what codependence is and how to move away from it. Excellent resource for 'parent' figures in parent/child dynamics.

Chabris, C., & Simons, D. (2010). *The invisible gorilla: And other ways our intuitions deceive us*. New York, NY: Crown.
Fascinating look at the *illusion of attention* and the *illusion of memory* (among others) that demonstrates that we can't trust the accuracy of either.

FDA drug safety communication: Safety reveiw update of medications used to treat ADHD in adults. (2011, December 12). Retrieved from http://www.fda.gov/Drugs/DrugSafety/ucm279858.htm

Fulbright, Y. K. (2009). *The better sex guide to extraordinary lovemaking*. Beverly, MA: Quiver.
Facts, pictures, ideas for improving desire, arousal and orgasm.

Gottman, J. M. (1999). *The marriage clinic*. New York, NY: W. W. Norton & Company.
For therapists. Marriage therapy theory based upon Gottman's research findings.

Gottman, J. M. (2011). *The science of trust: Emotional attunement for couples*. New York, NY: W. W. Norton.
Based in his research on trust and repair, Gottman offers a specific therapeutic approach to getting through negative emotional events that he calls "Attunement."

Gottman, J. M., & Silver, N. (1999). *The seven principles for making marriage work*. New York, NY: Three Rivers Press.
Written for couples. Provides an overview of important research findings plus exercises to incorporate key ideas into your relationship.

Hallowell, E., & Ratey, J. (n.d.). About Dyslexia: Symptoms; Signs; Statistics; and a Personal Story. Retrieved January 2, 2014, from http://www.additudemag.com/adhd/article/799.html

Hallowell, E. M. (2004). *Dare to forgive*. Deerfield Beach, FL: Health Communications.
Explores the nature of true forgiveness and why it is a strength and gift to forgive yourself and others.

Hallowell, E. M. (2006). CrazyBusy: Overstretched, overbooked, and about to snap! New York, NY: Ballantine.

Hallowell, E. M., & Jensen, P. S. (2008). *Superparenting for ADD: An innovative approach to raising your distracted child.* New York, NY: Ballantine.

Information on mirror traits, among other things. Written for parents of children with ADHD.

Hallowell, E. M., & Ratey, J. J. (2005). *Delivered from distraction: Getting the most out of life with attention deficit disorder.* New York, NY: Ballantine.

Inspirational look at adult ADHD and how to live your life fully with it by two of the world's experts on ADHD.

Hatfield, E., Sprecher, S., Pillemer, J. T., Greenberger, D., & Wexler, P. (1988). Gender differences in what is desired in the sexual relationship. *Journal of Psychology & Human Sexuality*, 1(2), 39-52.

Kohlberg, J., & Nadeau, K. (2002). *ADD-friendly ways to organize your life*. New York, NY: Routledge.

One of the best books available about how to get organized when you have ADHD.

Lerner, H. (2005). *The dance of anger: A woman's guide to changing the patterns of intimate relationships*. New York, NY: HarperCollins.

The classic about how to step out of the cycle of anger and create lasting improvements in your life.

Lerner, H. G. (1989). *The dance of intimacy: A woman's guide to courageous acts of change in key relationships*. New York, NY: Harper & Row.

How to build intimacy in all relationships. Covers overfunctioning and underfunctioning relevant for parent/child interactions.

Levitin, D. (2013, February 8). What you might be missing: Startling stories about how our minds work can too easily neglect the bigger picture. Retrieved January 3, 2014, from http://online.wsj.com/news/articles/SB10001424127887323829504578272241035441214

Review of the book, *Blindspot*

Mason, O. (n.d.). *When two meds are better than one: Combination medication management for ADHD* [PowerPoint presentation]. Retrieved from http://www.attentionmd.com/

Presented at 2013 CHADD conference on 11/9/13. Symptom reduction studies cited specifically in presentation.

Melby-Lervag, M., & Hulme, C. (2013, March). Can working memory training ameliorate ADHD and other learning disorders? A systematic meta-analytic review. The ADHD Report, 21(2), 1-5.

Niederhofer, H. (n.d.). Association of attention deficity hyperactivity disorder and celiac disease: A brief report. Retrieved January 2, 2014, from http://www.ncbi.nlm.nih.gov/pubmed/21977364

Orlov, M. C. (Ed.). (n.d.). Hope for the hopeless. Retrieved from ADHD and marriage: learning to thrive in your relationship website: http://www.ADHDmarriage.com

Forum post submitted by 'irrelephant.'

Orlov, M. C. (2010). *The ADHD effect on marriage: Understand and rebuild your relationship in six steps*. Plantation, FL: Specialty Press.

Award-winning introduction to how ADHD impacts adult relationships.

Orlov, M. C. (2013, October 30). *The ADHD effect in-depth couple's seminar written Q&A (multiple sessions).* Unpublished manuscript.

Questions written by seminar participants, answered in writing by Melissa Orlov. Multiple course session materials used.

Parker, C. (2010). *ADHD medication rules: Brain science & common sense*. Koehlerbooks.

Parker-Pope, T. (2008, February 12). Reinventing date night for long-married couples. *New York Times*.

Parker-Pope, T. (2010). *For better: The science of a good marriage.* New York, NY: Dutton.

Explores what the science says about romance, marriage and sex. A very interesting book that explores the elements of a good marriage.

Parker-Pope, T. (2010, May 10). The science of a happy marriage. Retrieved January 6, 2014, from http://well.blogs.nytimes.com/2010/05/10/tracking-the-science-of-commitment/

Ratey, J. (2013, December 2). [E-mail to M. Orlov].

Smoking and ADHD: What's the connection? (n.d.). Retrieved January 2, 2014, from http://www.help4adhd.org/faq.cfm?fid=44&varLang=en

Sonuga-Barke, E. J.S., Brandeis, D., Cortese, S., Ferrin, M., Holtmann, M., Stevenson, J., . . . European ADHD Guidelines Group. (2013). Nonpharmacological interventions for ADHD: Systematic review and meta-analyses of randomized controlled trials of dietary and psychological treatments. *American Journal of Psychiatry, 170*(3), 275-289.

TED Talks (Producer). (2008, October). *Mihaly Csikszentmihalyi: Flow, the secret to happiness.* Podcast retrieved from http://www.ted.com/talks/mihaly_csikszentmihalyi_on_flow.html

From a 2004 TED talk, posted in 2008.

Tuckman, A. (2009). *More attention, less deficit: Success strategies for adults with ADHD.* Plantation, FL: Specialty Press.

Complete overview of adult ADHD, with many helpful strategies for how to manage it.

Tuckman, A. (2012). U*nderstand your brain, get more done: The ADHD executive functions workbook.* Plantation, FL: Specialty Press.

Explores the executive functions involved with ADHD, and provides worksheets and ideas for becoming more consistent and effective.

Weiner-Davis, M. (2003). *The sex-starved marriage: Boosting your marriage libido.* New York, NY: Simon & Schuster.

For couples in which one partner is dissatisfied with the quantity of sex in the relationship.

Westheimer, R. K., & Lehu, P. (2001). *Rekindling romance for dummies.* Hoboken, NJ: Wiley.

Dr. Ruth gives lots of tips and ideas for rekindling romance in this easy-to-read back to basics book.

Index

D

T

Notes

Notes

Notes